This book belongs to

_____

FINDING
GOD'S
PATH
THROUGH YOUR
TRIALS

Elizabeth George

HARVEST HOUSE PUBLISHERS

EUGENE, OREGON

Cover photo © Gary Yeowell / Photographer's Choice / Getty Images

Cover by Dugan Design Group, Bloomington, Minnesota

FINDING GOD'S PATH THROUGH YOUR TRIALS
Copyright © 2007 by Elizabeth George
Published by Harvest House Publishers
Eugene, Oregon 97402
www.harvesthousepublishers.com

Library of Congress Cataloging-in-Publication Data
  George, Elizabeth, 1944-
  Finding God's path through your trials / Elizabeth George.
     p. cm.
  ISBN-13: 978-0-7369-1374-4 (pbk.)
  ISBN-10: 0-7369-1374-2 (pbk.)
  1. Suffering—Biblical teaching. 2. Consolation—Biblical teaching. 3. Christian
women—Religious life. I. Title.
  BS680.S854G46 2007
  248.8'6—dc22
                                            2007012043

Printed in the United States of America

    07 08 09 10 11 12 13 14 15 / VP-SK / 12 11 10 9 8 7 6 5 4 3 2 1

Contents

Section 4 — Becoming a Mighty Woman

Section 5 — Becoming an Enduring Woman

A Final Word

A Word About Trials

≈

A daughter's health and needed brain scan.
A soldier deploying to a war zone.
A couple with a son going through problems.
A suicidal daughter.
A dying dad.
A lack of self-control and/or addiction.

Whether we like it or not, trials and tribulation are part of our everyday lives. I can still remember reading John 16:33 as a new Christian making my way through the New Testament. In words spoken to His disciples, Jesus boldly stated, "In the world you *will* have tribulation." At that time I believed that everything would get better, that being a Christian would surely one day mean a problem-free life. However, the truth is that you and I—and everyone else—*will* suffer. We live in a sinful, fallen world that involves bodies deteriorating, relationships that require attention, temptation coming from every direction, and relentless persecution of believers because of their testimony for Christ.

As you read through this book, you will encounter some wisdom from the Bible about trials...and about how you can approach them. You will also learn how others have handled trials and how their examples—along with God's grace—can help you manage your way through your own set of trials. Regardless of what happens to you along life's way, keep these words from Jesus in your mind and heart. On the heels of His statement regarding the universality of trials and tribulation, Jesus said, "Be of good cheer, I have overcome the world" (John 16:33).

This is God's good news! Christ's victory, accomplished through His death and resurrection, rendered the world's opposition null and void. Yes, we will suffer, fall, fail, and be attacked. We will experience trials of every magnitude and every length of duration, from being locked out of the car until help arrives to a life-altering trial with no end or change in sight. But Christ's triumph has already guaranteed a smashing defeat of the world and its evil, including our trials.

As we talk about finding God's path through your trials, keep these words from the apostle Paul handy in your heart:

- ❦ "But thanks be to God, who gives us the victory through our Lord Jesus Christ" (1 Corinthians 15:57).

- ❦ "Yet in all these things we are more than conquerors through Him who loved us" (Romans 8:37).

- ❦ "Blessed be the God and Father of our Lord Jesus Christ, the Father of mercies and God of all comfort, who comforts us in all our tribulation" (2 Corinthians 1:3-4).

Section 1

Becoming a Joyful Woman

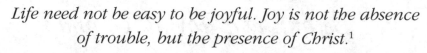

Life need not be easy to be joyful. Joy is not the absence of trouble, but the presence of Christ.[1]

WILLIAM VANDER HOVEN

1

Accepting the Truth

❧

My brethren, count it all joy
when you fall into various trials.

James 1:2

Have you ever been asked to do something you weren't too excited about? Something that might even cause some pain physically, mentally, or emotionally? Probably fairly often, right? Well, that happened to me one summer morning. One of my phone calls that sunny day was from the woman who chaired the women's ministry at my family's church. She asked me to pray about teaching the women's Bible study group the following spring. And not only was she asking me to pray about leading the group, but she actually gave me the topic of the Bible study—"trials" of all things! Her committee had discussed the needs among women in the church and decided that the topic of successfully handling trials would be important since so many were experiencing difficulties in some form or another.

Well, little did these ladies know, but their request quickly became a trial in my life. Why, you ask? Read on!

My first response to this woman, I'm sorry to say, was negative. I don't like to teach by assignment. I much prefer to instruct out of the overflow of my own personal study of the Bible.

My second response, I'm also sorry to say, was fear. Who would want to attend a class that majored on problems? Don't most people want to hear pleasant, happy things? I certainly didn't want to be a teacher of doom and gloom!

But as I talked it over with God, He changed my heart. I accepted the opportunity as coming from Him...that *He* was asking me to address the everyday, every-person exposure to trouble, and that He had some things to teach me. The church committee was indeed wise: Trials are part of life, including mine...and yours.

Looking to Another Teacher

Once I worked through the trial of doing something I wasn't sure I wanted to do and accepted the challenge of diving into the topic of trials, my mind raced to James, the writer of the book of James in the Bible. I thought James might have had a similar experience because he taught about trials.

Imagine yourself in James' position. He was given an assignment to teach a course that could have been entitled "Trials 101." Knowing that all Christians suffer, the president of the college—God Himself—asked James to create curriculum that would give all Christians the basics needed for handling bad times.

Oh, but that's not all! James was essentially told the class would have to be a *correspondence* course. Why? Because he would never meet or talk to the people who needed and "studied" this course designed to help them manage their problems and challenges. Therefore James' assignment was to write instructions that were universal—that would help in *any* and *every* situation for *all* time. He was to put in writing information that would aid *any* and *every*

Christian, from the babe in Christ facing initial growing pains to the seasoned saint on his or her deathbed. He was to communicate guidelines that would instruct God's people in how to handle everything from a small insult to a major catastrophe.

What would you do if you were James? What would you say? Where would you start? My friend, this is exactly the assignment God gave to James. There were some saints "out there" who needed help. Jewish believers living outside Jerusalem and Palestine, outside the hub of Christianity, were confronting a variety of trials. James' job was to give them advice on how to deal with their problems in a godly way.

And what were the results of God's assignment to James? Here are a few facts surrounding James' timeless lessons to all believers on how to find God's path through trials.

Getting Straight to the Point

To begin, the book of James is the first New Testament epistle (letter) written, dated just 15 years after the death of Christ. It is a bold, straight-to-the-point, practical manual on holy living under any and all conditions—including distress. Filled with wisdom, the epistle of James has been likened to the book of Proverbs because of its short, razor-sharp statements regarding godly living.

How did James fulfill his assignment from God? He sat down and, under the inspiration of the Holy Spirit, wrote lists of advice for his unseen readers—a catalog of principles, of do's and don'ts, of rules to live by. He gave his brothers and sisters in Christ words of wisdom for all circumstances.

And why was James chosen to do this? Possibly because he was the half-brother of Jesus (see Matthew 13:55). You see, James—a younger sibling in the household—would have witnessed firsthand how Jesus, the Son of God and the Perfect Man, handled trials.

Now pretend you're James. What would you say to begin your course billed as "Trials 101"? The greeting card industry would probably say to the poor, suffering saints: "Thinking of you" or "Get well soon!" or "Hang in there, baby!" Some psychology books would suggest to these problem-ridden people that they could withdraw, seek to win, fight, give in, or compromise. Amazingly, James' course in The School of Trials offered advice differing vastly from these sentiments and counsel. In just nine words, James dove right in, got straight to the point, and issued a command:

Count it all joy...when you fall into various trials
(James 1:2).

Bypassing all triviality, small talk, words of introduction, and sugarcoating, James exhorted his readers to face their trials head-on and take a positive approach—to *rejoice* in their troubles! Sound impossible? It is...unless we understand several truths about trials.

Trials Are a Fact of Life

Life isn't easy. And being a Christian isn't easy either. Sure, we have newness of life in Christ and our assurances from God. But as believers we can expect to be jostled by trials all along the way:

❧ Peter told his readers: "Do not think it strange concerning the fiery trial which is to try you, as though some strange thing happened to you" (1 Peter 4:12).

❧ Paul wrote that "all who desire to live godly in Christ Jesus will suffer persecution" (2 Timothy 3:12).

❧ Jesus taught that "in the world you will have tribulation" (John 16:33).

We can be sure trials will hit us. All kinds of experiences will come to us, including negative ones. But *when* they arrive, says James, we have choices to make. One of those choices is attitude. God allows us the privilege of choosing our attitude. We can be bitter, angry, disgruntled, or depressed. It's up to us. Or we can choose to be women who sigh…and sigh…and sigh in defeat some more. We can slump, scowl, sulk, and complain.

But James recommends a better way, a better outlook to choose—indeed, the best way! He shares with us the right choice. He encourages us to decide to have a joyful attitude. *James' first rule for joyful living in unjoyful circumstances is to "count it all joy."*

Learning to Count

Just as the ABCs are basic to learning how to read, so a knowledge of the 1-2-3s is fundamental to learning how to triumph in trials. James' elementary, bare-bones course on godly endurance in suffering includes learning to count. He says *"count it all joy"* when you encounter every trial. Whenever I read these words, my immediate reaction is to not like them. God's words through James are unexpected and shocking, like ice water thrown in my face. Why? Because I want James (and everyone!) to

> *Counting trials as joy is a matter of faith, not feelings.*

identify with me, to feel my pain. I want empathy and sympathy. I want someone to cut me some slack. I want someone to woo me into a godly attitude.

However, because an obedient heart is something I desire (and I'm thinking you do too), I realize that I have to learn to count instead of counting on others. To "count" means to evaluate, to consider, and to account for something. In the case of James 1, verse 2, it is *the trial that is to be evaluated to the point that a* decision *is made to "count" it as all joy.* To "count" involves careful, deliberate judgment. In the end, we are supposed to look at the trial—whatever it is—and count it as *joy.*

I have learned several things about this "counting." First, counting a trial as joy is done with the mind...not the emotions. It is a matter of faith, not of feelings. It is a mental discipline. And it is an issue of sheer obedience. God is not asking Christians who are involved in trials to "feel" joy. No, He is asking them to follow His instructions and "count" (to evaluate, consider, determine, and decide) those trials to be joy.

And second, counting trials as joy has nothing to do with the body or how a Christian is feeling physically. Counting eliminates evaluations according to physical experience against the idea that "if it feels good, it is a good thing," "if it feels bad, it must be a bad thing" notions.

Christians, therefore, are not to "count" or evaluate their trials according to looks or feelings. Counting is done not by sight, but *by faith* (2 Corinthians 5:7). By faith and in obedience we *choose* to count any and every trial as joy. Why? Because that's what God says we must do to find His path through our trials.

—*Taking a Step Forward*—

Where does today find you? Where do you reside, and do you want to be there or like being there? For a woman, many times the place she resides is not her ideal. For instance, if you are married, you may follow your husband as he leads you halfway around the world...or maybe he desires to make no moves at all while you're itching for a new start. You leave family—sisters, brothers, parents, married children, grandchildren, and friends—behind as you cleave to your husband. Like Sarah in the Old Testament (Genesis 12:1-5), you may have to leave behind all that is familiar and friendly to taste that which is different and what may not seem beneficial at the time to you and your family.

And if you're single, you experience loss as your job takes you from place to place, tearing you away from loved ones, a good church, and your support system. It may seem like you're starting over...and over...and over again.

My friend, these are trials.

And in what state of mind or spirit does today find you? Are you suffering from sorrow, discouragement, fear, anxiety, worry, loneliness, or despair? Even the powerful warrior King David had his days of dismay. He had his problems with people. David cried out to God, "Have mercy on me, O LORD! Consider my trouble from those who hate me" (Psalm 9:13). He had times when he thought he would surely die: "I would have lost heart, unless I had believed that I would see the goodness of the LORD" (Psalm 27:13).

> *You can be a joyful woman regardless of the problems you face.*

Can you relate? Is any issue or problem—a relationship, an illness, a life circumstance—troubling you today? More than likely the answer is yes. You can take a giant, positive step forward by realizing the truth that trials are a fact of life. Don't get blown away by trials. Don't wonder *why* something happened to you. Don't accuse God of evil with thoughts like *How could a loving God let this happen?* Don't doubt God, wondering, *Where is God when I need Him?* or *Where was God when this happened?*

And please don't give in to anger, depression, and discouragement. And don't decide, "Well, I'll just drop out of this race. I give up! I can't go on. In fact, I don't even want to go on."

And don't put off a positive attitude, thinking, *When the pain eases up, I'll be more joyful* or *When this is over, I'll be happy again. Then I'll have joy.*

Instead, acknowledge the truth that trials are part of life on this planet. Follow God's advice through James and "count it all joy." Make the right choice of attitude—the one God prescribes. Bow your knee, your heart, and your emotions before God Almighty and express your heart attitude: "God, I don't like this, but You say I am to count this trouble as joy. Therefore, by Your grace, I am choosing to do so."

Will you do this? Accepting the truth about trials makes all the difference in your day, in your hardships, and especially in your life! This is God's path through your trials. You can be a joyful woman in your problems and regardless of your problems.

Just as the stars shine brightest in the darkest night,
so your joy blazes brilliantly through
life's worst problems when you count them as joy.[1]

2

Using an Easy Sorting System

҉

Consider it all joy, my brethren,
when you encounter various trials.

James 1:2 NASB

҉ One wonderful day when all was well—one of those rare,
perfect days—I almost skipped to the mailbox. I opened
it up to see what treasures lay within (you know, new magazine
issues, the fall clothing catalogs, the Wal-Mart flyer highlighting
the next sale). And there at the curb in front of my house I "fell
into" a challenging trial. A letter informed me that as a teacher in
our church I was required to participate in an upcoming, nine-
month ministry training course. There were no ifs, ands, or buts.
If I wanted to continue in my present areas of service, I would
have to attend.

Immediately I reacted. Where was the time going to come from?
I was already too busy! Where could I possibly dig up the hours
to not only attend the classes and half-day training sessions, but
also to do the extensive homework?

Now...what did James say to do about something like this? Oh yes, I should count it all joy.

Inside my home I sat down before God and laid out my problem, my trial. I looked at my calendar and panicked. I prayed. I cried. I debated with God, pulling out every "Yes, but..." and "What about..." I could think of. I wrote a letter asking to be excused from the mandatory training...and then tore it up. Next I wrote a letter of resignation from my ministries in protest.

Needless to say, it was horrible...and I was horrible. And, as I'm sure you can tell, I was a mess. I'll let you know in a minute how my ordeal ended...

Right now let me share more wisdom from God through James about how to find your path through whatever trial lies in front of you, through whatever trouble may be spoiling your glorious day. It helped me, and it will help you too. And believe it or not, it had to do with bookkeeping, with learning and using a simple, easy sorting system.

The Bookkeeping Principle

Is bookkeeping a nightmare for you? For many the activity of keeping track of financial affairs could well hold the Number One spot on their list of "Least Favorite Things to Do." You probably understand enough about bookkeeping to know that it is tedious, time-consuming, often frustrating work. You may also wonder, "So what's the big deal about keeping track of money anyway? Sooner or later my credit-card bill will come in the mail. Then I'll know at a glance how I spent my money...of which there is never enough anyway."

The truth is, bookkeeping is a meaningful discipline. We gain peace of mind when we know exactly what we have and don't have in the Money Department. We can chart our financial path for the day, month, and year depending on what we have or don't have. We can know precisely what we have or need in order to provide for ourselves and others, to move forward on our plans and dreams, and, most importantly, to serve our Lord.

Well, I have some good news for you. Even a little experience with bookkeeping or some basic accounting knowledge is useful in grasping God's command to count trials as joy. Picturing a bookkeeper in your mind will help you comprehend James' advice on how to manage your trials God's way. You will benefit from the mind-set of a bookkeeper as you approach your trials. Like an accountant who records the transactions of a business, you can do better "business" with God as you seek to please Him.

Debit or Credit?

Maybe my own bookkeeping story will help explain what I mean. In our household I learned (yes, learned!) as a new bride to be a bookkeeper when my husband, Jim, left for six months to go to army boot camp. During his absence I devised a system that was not very sophisticated. I used a shoebox and put all the bills and receipts into it each day. I also purchased a pad of green ledger sheets at an office supply store. Each page in the ledger pad had two columns, one labeled "debit" and one labeled "credit."

Believe it or not, there are only a few fundamental rules to follow for bookkeeping and accounting, and sticking to those guidelines makes bookkeeping a meticulous and precise—and easy!—discipline. One rule is that every amount of money is either a debit or a credit. It is either an expense or income. It is either a loss or a gain, a liability or an asset.

Because there are only two columns on the accountant's basic bookkeeping page—debit and credit—the job of the bookkeeper is to determine whether each amount of money being handled is a debit or a credit. Armed with the mind-set of an accountant and this rule of bookkeeping, the bookkeeper makes a conscious decision where to record each entry.

I regularly reached into the shoebox, pulled out one piece of

> *You have to decide whether to count each difficulty as joy or sorrow.*

paper, and made a decision about which category it belonged to on the ledger page. I had to ask of each amount, each receipt, each payment: "Are you a debit or a credit?" If money went out, it was a debit and put in the debit column. If money came in, it was a credit and put in the credit column. It's like the check register in the back of your checkbook. Take a look at it. You'll find these same two columns, and every amount of money you deal with is accounted for in one or the other of these two columns.

"Counting" (considering, reckoning, accounting, evaluating, or—my personal favorite—chalking-up) trials as "joy" is very much the same discipline. You (and I) have to do the bookkeeping, so to speak, and make a very conscious decision about each of your troubles. You have to decide whether to count each individual difficulty as *joy* or to count it as *sorrow*. These are the only two options available for your spiritual bookkeeping. As you hold each problem up before God for His clerical assistance, you may find yourself saying to Him, "Lord, this trial doesn't *look* like joy, and it certainly doesn't *feel* like joy. I can't imagine how in the world this thing is ever going to turn out to *be* joy. But based on Your divine rules for bookkeeping, I will count this trial as joy."

Then you obediently take pen in hand and decisively, in a willful act, mark your trial in the "joy" column. That's how the decision is made to count your trial as joy, as a credit, as an asset, as income…as a positive!

Reacting or Yielding?

Now, to share the results of my personal experience, the one I encountered at the mailbox about the church training course. Once I remembered God's instructions for managing trials—to count them all joy—I tore up my letter of appeal and my note of resignation. In my heart I knew these were reactions, not the actions God was asking me to take. All He was asking me to do was to "count it all joy." He was looking for a *godly* response, a *mature* response, a *joyous* response—*His* response! But how was I to do this?

By His grace I quieted myself and my mind and my emotions. And I dipped the cold, steel tip of my spiritual bookkeeping pen into the ink of obedience. With God's enablement, I chose to place this trial into the "joy" column. I yielded to His imperative command to be joyful. Again, with God's help, I used my mind and will to override my feelings and emotions and, willfully, with hand and heart, I recorded this seemingly unfair, undesirable, stress-producing, surprise demand (in short, a trial!) in the "joy" column. At last I "counted it all joy."

I can tell you that going through this decision-making process and yielding to God's choice for me—the choice to count trials as joy—made a profound difference in my attitude. I was able to throw myself wholeheartedly into the lengthy sessions *and* the reading *and* the homework *and* the training by following God's instructions for managing trials in James 1:2. He showed me the path—*God's* path—through my challenge. Plus, as a divine bonus, through the coursework I learned valuable biblical instructions that helped me grow in a multitude of ways as a Christian. This resulted in a stronger ministry to the women God allows me to meet.

Doing It Daily

I can also tell you that my struggle with my trial in no way stopped with the singular act of counting that one trial as joy that one time. No, it was not a once-for-all decision that lasted through the months. Oh no! At least once daily for *many* months I had to decide again and again and again to "count it all joy."

> *A daily time of sitting before God with your spiritual ledger sheet and taking each trial in hand one by one is vital.*

Just as I learned the hard way to handle my financial bookkeeping daily, I learned to handle my difficulties daily. For instance, if I save up my financial bookkeeping, I get behind and lose track of our finances. I become overwhelmed by the number of accounting items that require attention. The time needed to handle the accumulated work after a time of neglect seems impossible to find. And I forget things—like paying a bill—and end up in the minus column. But if I do my financial bookkeeping daily, I'm always on top of things. There is no needless waste of money or emotion.

It's the same with my personal accounting of the trials in my life. If I handle my trials daily, holding them up before God and examining each one with Him in prayer, and then obediently do the bookkeeping of counting each one in the joy column, I am less likely to be overwhelmed or let one slip by.

This is why a daily time of sitting before God with your spiritual ledger sheet and taking each trial in hand one by one is vital. I encourage you to have a daily time of prayer, a daily time of spiritual accounting. A joyful woman is one who deals daily with her problems, faithfully and obediently placing her troubles in the joy column…over and over again. Even though tears may fall and mark the ledger sheet, the act of counting and evaluating our trials as joys makes a difference—all the difference, in fact!

Persevering Through Pain

Whenever I am tempted to feel especially sorry for myself or to think no one is suffering as much as I am or in the same way, I take a fresh look at the man named Job in the Old Testament. Job was godly, blameless, and righteous. He worked hard and prayed faithfully. He was an exemplary father. He sought to obey God on all points. Yet his faith in God was tested with severe physical, financial, and spiritual trials. Job blazed a trail for all who are subjected to problems as he persevered through his pain. In the end, this man who declared, "Blessed be the name of the LORD" (Job 1:21) during his trials was magnificently blessed by the Lord (42:12).

Because of the grace of God we can be strong even when suffering weakens us.

One of my favorite scriptures—2 Corinthians 12:10—clearly teaches there are many kinds of pain. This verse cites the triumphant words of the apostle Paul as he closes his thoughts on his own personal suffering—on his "thorn in the flesh" (verse 7). After hearing Jesus' words of promise concerning His all-sufficient grace for enduring distress, Paul announced, "Therefore I take pleasure...

> ...in infirmities [weaknesses],
>
> ...in reproaches [insults and ill-treatment],
>
> ...in needs [hardships and deprivations],
>
> ...in persecutions [torment],
>
> ...in distresses [difficulties and times of difficulty]"
> (2 Corinthians 12:10).

Think about it. Paul lists five different types of suffering, five different kinds of adversity. And, as Bible scholars note, the list is not complete in reference to Paul's trials. This means we are never the only ones suffering. Suffering takes on many faces, but it is universal to humankind due to the fall of Adam in the garden of Eden (Genesis 3:1-7).

But the good news is we can persevere through pain. Because of the grace of God we can be strong even when suffering weakens us. By keeping James' command to "count it all joy" and by following Paul's example of rejoicing in the power of Christ (2 Corinthians 12:9-10), you and I can triumph over our ordeals. And, like Job, we know blessings await us on the other side of each trial.

—Taking a Step Forward—

A path or walkway is a functional addition to any yard or garden. And your life too becomes more orderly and easily navigated when you have a path to follow. As you walk through life and its sure-to-come trials, your day and your life are benefited and eased by the path God has designed for you to tread upon. Pain and trouble and suffering are a path you must walk, so why not beautify and streamline it with God's gracious joy? As James advises, When you fall into trials, don't fall off God's path through them. Instead, become a bookkeeper and "count it all joy."

Are there "impossible" demands being put upon you right now? Any difficulty that causes you sorrow? Any surprise developments in a relationship? Any little issues that are unsettling, a bother, a nuisance, that can so easily rob you of your joy? Be thankful! Be joyful! There is hope. There is a way through these—and all— trials. God makes it possible for you to find His way, His path, His peace, and His joy through everything. It is to these trials of life that James speaks. The sovereign solution, according to God, regardless of the complexity of any difficulty, is simple: "Count it all joy."

God calls you to set aside your feelings, fears, and emotions and willfully decide to count all trials as joy, no matter what they are. Blessings stand on the other side of heeding James' simple advice to make a conscious commitment to face your tough issues with joy...to choose to be joyful. Blessings awaited Job on the other side of his many ordeals. And blessings were mine in my situation once I yielded to God's counsel to count my trial of attending ministry teaching classes as joy and chose to approach it with a joyful attitude.

Following God's bookkeeping guidelines and using His easy sorting system perfects and completes us and makes us grow in patience. James 1:2-4 says: "My brethren, count it all joy when you fall into various trials, knowing that the testing of your faith produces patience. But let patience have its perfect work, that you may be perfect and complete, lacking nothing." Persevering through trials causes us to bear fruit. One of those fruits is the beauty of being a joyful woman…no matter what is going on or what is lacking in your life. This is one of God's steps to finding and staying on His path. Handling your trials *His way* by evaluating them to be joy is *the way* to make it through your difficulties with an unexplainable contentment that brings honor and glory to Him.

How strong is your faith and trust in God? Your trials and difficulties are a golden opportunity for joy. You *can* face your problems with a positive outlook! You *can* be joyful even when your whole world seems to be falling apart! How? You know the answer by now: Count it all joy. This puts you on God's path through your trials.

*Christ is not only a remedy for your weariness
and trouble, but He will give you an abundance of
the contrary, [of] joy and delight.*

Jonathan Edwards

3

Evaluating What's Happening

❦

Consider it pure joy, my brothers,
whenever you face trials of many kinds.

James 1:2 NIV

❦ Everyone encounters and experiences trials. But the women enrolled in my evening Bible course on the book of James taught me new depths of trials as we began looking for God's path through them. When we finished studying James, chapter 1, on the first night of class, I gave this assignment: For one week keep a journal of your trials, how you chose to count them as joy, and any results.

I was in no way prepared for this homework project to be life-changing for the ladies or for them to take it so seriously. The next week most of the papers turned in were at least five pages in length. The students listed *all* their trials, keeping track of each full day for a full week.

One woman's paper really caused my heart to break as she shared her Number One problem. Her husband had received a job promotion that meant moving their children, possessions, and pets across the country. To make the move to California she had to give up her home, her church, her family, and her friends.

Within weeks of their major move, this husband and father chose to abandon his family, leaving this dear woman bereft as a single mom and a stranger in a strange land. And now her Bible class assignment was to count *all* her trials as *all* joy for an entire week! She wondered if she could do it. If she could handle it.

I'll let you in on more of her story in a few minutes, but for now let's go back to my Bible class—back to school!

Viewing Trials the Wrong Way

One evening I asked these women in my night class, "What are some ways people mistakenly view or respond to trials?" Just look at the variety of flawed, unscriptural thoughts and mistaken responses they came up with!

- ❧ Thinking God must be punishing me: "What have I done now?"

- ❧ Thinking God must be judging me: "God must be mad at me."

- ❧ Thinking God has forgotten me: "He's turned His back. He's not looking. I'm not important to Him."

- ❧ Thinking I must be inferior to others: "I'm not as good as other Christians. That's why I have to suffer like this."

- ❧ Thinking the trial has to do with God's lack of love: "God doesn't love me anymore."

- ❧ Thinking the trial is something to get out of, hurry through, or manipulate: "Quick, how can I end this?"

❧ Thinking the trial is something to be ashamed of: "What will others think? If anyone finds out, it will hurt my reputation."

Faulty thinking like these examples can lead to faulty responses such as these:

❧ Wondering "why me?": "It only happens to me!"

❧ Placing the blame on others: "It's someone else's fault."

❧ Blaming Satan: "The devil did this."

❧ Questioning God: "Why, Lord? What are You doing? What's wrong with me? What's wrong in my life?"

❧ Sinking into depression: "Where is my sackcloth? And where can I get my hands on some ashes?"

❧ Cowering in dread and fear, afraid to take a step or make a move: "I don't dare go out of the house. Something else might happen to me."

❧ Getting angry at God, others, and self: "How could You do this to me? I'm fed up with these people. I never do anything right. Forget this Christianity thing!"

❧ Marveling in disbelief: "I thought being a Christian meant being happy and having a trouble-free life."

❧ Reacting in frustration: "This is ridiculous. I can live a better life without this."

❧ Attributing evil to God by thinking He enjoys our suffering: "Are You having fun yet, God?"

- ใ Discounting the trial: "It's just fate, coincidence, something that just happened, a bit of bad luck."

- ใ Limiting God: "I know He knows and cares, but I guess He just isn't able to keep these things from happening...or maybe He's unable to stop it."

- ใ Viewing trials as an interference or interruption or irritation: "It's just a pesky problem that has to be endured."

Hopefully by now you've decided to follow God's sure instructions for managing and enduring trials—for finding His path through your trials and gloriously walking it. And if you've been guilty of some of these faulty evaluations about your trials and some of the listed responses, please know you are not alone. The women in my class and I came up with these lists from personal experiences!

I know God's grace will enable you to look at your trials from His viewpoint. Are you following through on God's instructions to count each trial as joy? Great! Now, what is the next step for being a joyful woman?

Knowing Genuine Joy

James gives it to us in ten words. He says not only are we to evaluate the contents of each trial as joy, but he adds one tiny word with a big message. He says, "Count it *all* joy when you fall into various trials" (James 1:2). *All* joy speaks of pure joy, unmixed joy, joy to the highest—genuine joy. We are exhorted to count each trial as nothing but joy. A godly woman will consider her trials to be *wholly joyful* even in the midst of sorrow.

As a woman does her spiritual bookkeeping, carefully analyzes and evaluates what's happening in her life, and willfully places each trial in the "joy" column, so she also determines that it is wholly joy—pure joy. She makes a decision to assess each trial as containing nothing but joy. This evaluation is done through the eyes of faith, *choosing* to evaluate each terrible or trivial trial as all—and nothing but—joy.

When I was a trainee in the evangelism program at my church, I memorized a number of Bible verses to use when sharing the gospel of Jesus Christ with others. One of those scriptures was Habakkuk 1:13. It's a statement about the person and nature of God that says, "You are of purer eyes than to behold evil, and cannot look on wickedness." In other words, God is too pure of eyes to behold *any* evil.[1]

To illustrate this verse those of us in the training sessions were told to imagine a gallon of pure white paint. Then we were to think about the fact that if one drop—just *one* drop—even a *partial* drop!—of any other color was put into that gallon of pure white paint, it would no longer be wholly white. Even if it was a drop of off-white, the gallon was no longer pure white.

With this example in mind, recall the image of the bookkeeper. He or she doesn't look at each amount of money and evaluate it on a sliding scale or stab at a guess. No, the single item is 100 percent a debit or 100 percent a credit. And you need the same mentality in evaluating your trials. Refuse to use any scale (for instance, a scale of one to ten) other than this 100 percent. Believe that each trial is always nothing but joy—pure joy. View your trials through eyes of faith and believe with a heart of faith that there is not one drop or hint of anything in your trials other than pure, unreserved, genuine, 100 percent joy!

> *View your trials through eyes of faith and believe with a heart of faith that there is only joy in them.*

This process of evaluation is a discipline. I recorded these words from my former pastor, John F. MacArthur, in my journal when he spoke regarding James, chapter 1, and the genuine joy that can be ours:

> Evaluating a trial as being joyful is something a Christian must discipline himself to do because joy is not the natural human response to troubles. He must make a conscious commitment to face each trial with a joyous attitude.

Rejoicing No Matter What

I have already mentioned the apostle Paul and his suffering. Look now at a small sample of his many miseries. In 2 Corinthians 11:23-27 Paul reports,

- ❧ "[I was...] in labors more abundant, in stripes above measure, in prisons more frequently, in deaths often. From the Jews five times I received forty stripes minus one.

- ❧ "Three times I was beaten with rods; once I was stoned; three times I was shipwrecked; a night and a day I have been in the deep;

- ❧ "[I was...] in journeys often, in perils of waters, in perils of robbers, in perils of my own countrymen, in perils of the Gentiles, in perils in the city, in perils in the wilderness, in perils in the sea, in perils among false brethren;

- ❧ "[I was...] in weariness and toil, in sleeplessness often, in hunger and thirst, in fastings often, in cold and nakedness."

Oh the suffering! The abuse! The perils! The treachery! Yet it was this Paul who spoke so often of joy. In the book of Philippians, sometimes referred to as the epistle of joy (which was written while Paul was in prison!), Paul exulted:

❧ "In this I rejoice, yes, and will rejoice" (Philippians 1:18).

❧ "Rejoice in the Lord" (3:1).

❧ "For we...rejoice in Christ Jesus" (3:3).

❧ "Rejoice in the Lord always. Again I will say, rejoice!" (4:4).

❧ "The God of peace will be with you" (4:9).

—*Taking a Step Forward* —

In landscaping there are many kinds of paths. One is a stepping-stone course that requires careful attention to stay on. Your assignment to count each trial as joy is one of the stones God carefully places to lead you along His path through your trials.

As I thought about genuine joy—*pure* joy, *unmixed* joy, *complete* and *total* joy, *sheer* joy, *all* joy—I realized I have a tendency to count a trial to be nine-tenths joy and reserve a special one-tenth of pain for myself. Something in me enjoys saving part of a problem for sorrow, for personal attention, for talking about with others, for self-pity, for nurturing a "martyr complex" or a "poor me" attitude, which I sometimes relish so much. I sometimes like feeling sorry for myself—at least a little! And yet here is my all-wise God, who promises me (and you!) "fullness of joy" and "pleasures forevermore" (Psalm 16:11), instructing me in no vague terms to count my testing as *all joy*.

Remember the student whose husband deserted her after their major move? This is how she evaluated her trials:

> If the Bible didn't tell me in James 1:2 to "count it all joy when you fall into various trials," I certainly would not be in the process of disciplining my mind in obedience as I am now. Because of the trial in my life at this time, I am searching the Lord's heart and mind and will and clinging [to Him] as never before. I am thankful that I've been told to do this—to count it all joy and to persevere in faith, otherwise the pain and hurt and confusion would be unbearable. As I depended upon this verse and others this week, I sought to obey and count the joys:
>
> ❧ I can see God's hand at work in my life in remarkable faithfulness as He speaks through those He loves and has called.
>
> ❧ I'm seeking to live the life He has called me to more fervently than I have ever done up till now.
>
> ❧ I'm learning His truths in a deeper way than I've ever known.
>
> ❧ I see relationships growing in areas I never would have chosen or expected, with great openings to share wherein my joy and strength comes.
>
> ❧ I can care more deeply for others who are hurting because now I know the hurt, the pain, the rejection.
>
> ❧ In some ways, I can more closely identify with the rejection Jesus endured and love Him more deeply.

My heart's desire is to be a mature Christian woman who is serving my God with my whole heart and mind and will. I consider it all joy that He loves me and cares enough for me to test and cause me to grow.

Here is a woman who is finding God's path through a terrible trial. I have to admit I almost feel envy as I see her strength and growth in the Lord. I want what she has. I desire the closeness to God and the powerful dependence on Him that she is experiencing. I want to be the truly joyful and mature woman she is becoming, a woman who focuses forward with full energy and unmingled joy despite extreme difficulties. If I could truly achieve this level of joy and maturity, any trial would be worth its pain.

> *Choose to follow God's beautiful and practical path through your trials!*

Do you desire to take growth steps forward? If so, try the assignment my women and I took on. For one week keep a journal of your trials. Then evaluate them from God's perspective, choose to count them as *all* joy, and record the positive results that come from making this godly choice. Choose to follow God's beautiful and practical path through your trials! He has carefully laid out the stepping-stones for you, the first one being a joyful attitude.

*Character cannot be developed in ease and quiet.
Only through experiences of trial and suffering
can the soul be strengthened, vision cleared,
ambition inspired and success achieved.*

HELEN KELLER

4

Expecting Bumps, Roadblocks, and Dead Ends

❧

Dear brothers and sisters,
whenever trouble comes your way,
let it be an opportunity for joy.

James 1:2 NLT

An enlightening book entitled *You Gotta Keep Dancin'* by Tim Hansel showed me a sobering treatment of trials from the author's firsthand experiences. The subtitle of the book is "In the Midst of Life's Hurts, You Can Choose Joy!" Mr. Hansel wrote about his personal suffering and those of others, presenting a powerful account of how God works in the midst of physical and emotional trauma. The thread that runs throughout his discussion of suffering and affliction is the importance of understanding that joy is a choice in and through pain.

Here's what happened to the author. Being a strong and physically fit man, Tim Hansel delighted in mountain climbing. On one of his climbs he fell quite a long way but was able to get up and make it down the mountain. As he drove himself home, he kept wondering, "Why am I so short? Why is the steering wheel so far away?"

It was only after Tim arrived home that he discovered the reason: His back was broken! (Talk about a bump, roadblock, and dead end!) Fortunately his body had gone into shock, enabling him to keep functioning and operating his car despite his injury until he got home safely. However, "home" now included 20-plus years of learning to live with chronic pain. It meant 20-plus years of realizing with each day and each stab of pain that disaster doesn't have to rob a person of joy in life.

Walking Through Your Ordeals

Have you heard of the five steps every person supposedly goes through after a loss or a great change or a trauma? The list goes like this:

❧ The first is denial, refusing to believe what has happened.

❧ Second is anger, the feeling of rage based on a frustration that cannot be satisfied.

❧ Third is bargaining, trying to make deals with God.

❧ Fourth is depression, a symptom of both pro-longed anger turned inward and of guilt.

❧ And, finally, fifth is acceptance. This positive stage is experienced when one realizes that what is is, it's not going to change, and it is truly real and will remain the same.[1]

Do you realize that when you handle your trials God's way, you can shortcut the first four reactions on this list (denial, anger, bargaining, depression) and fast-forward straight to acceptance? This is accomplished by "counting it all joy" when you fall into various trials. When you do, you rush to the place of joyful acceptance. "The fruit of the Spirit is…joy" (Galatians 5:22), and counting your trials as joy leads to bearing the Spirit's fruit in your life. To "walk in the Spirit" (verse 16) through your trials, you must choose joy.

Think again about Tim Hansel and his journey toward accepting and living with persistent pain. In his book he shared about meeting with Joni Eareckson Tada to interview her about the fact that she could feel nothing, including pain, due to a broken neck suffered as a teenager. He reported that after the interview with Joni was over, his little son came up to him, jumped into his lap, and gave him a big old hug. The crushing hug hurt terribly, but Tim surmised, "Wow! I'll take the pain because I can have this too!" In his process of learning to bear and deal with pain, Mr. Hansel wrote:

> If we are to have…joy in our lives, we must first discover what it looks like. It is not a feeling, it is a choice. It is not based on circumstances, it is based on attitude. It is free, but it is not cheap. It is the byproduct of a growing relationship with Jesus Christ. It is a promise, not a deal that we make with God. It is available to us when we make ourselves available to Him. It is something that we can receive by invitation and by choice. It requires commitment, courage, and endurance.[2]

These insights are from Hansel's section entitled "Choose Joy." In this portion of his book he emphasizes over and over that we are to *choose* joy, to count our trials as all joy.

Encountering Trials

We've discussed trials and our reactions to them, but now let's turn a corner and look at the trials themselves. James gives us two important facts about difficulties.

First, in the words of James, you will *"fall into* various trials" (James 1:2). Imagine your Christian life as a board game. Maybe the game is called "The Path to Perfection" or "Moving Toward Maturity." As you play the game, you are merrily moving your little token around the board. It's your turn to draw instructions and see what your next move will be. Maybe the card allows you to advance five steps with no obstacles, or pass your next exam, or pass by other players and get that promotion, or meet Mr. Wonderful, or get a bonus turn (a surprise refund or check in the mail). Or maybe the instructions tell you to spend one turn in the hospital, lose a turn for no reason at all, hold back and watch others pass you by, or do not collect a tax refund this year but instead have taxes due. With a draw like any of these, you have "fallen into" a trial.

> *Trials are not punishments from God, and they are not consequences of sin (although sin can lead to trials).*

"Fall into." This concept means to encounter, to meet up with, to bump into, to drop into the midst of something, to find yourself surrounded or enveloped in something. It indicates that encountering trials is not merely a possibility but an inevitability. In other words, trials are a certainty. They are part of daily life on earth.

Jesus' parable of the Good Samaritan illustrates the meaning of *falling into* a trial (Luke 10:30-37). In this story "a certain man went down from Jerusalem to Jericho, and *fell among* thieves" (verse 30). There it is! This man was simply going about his business, moving along the road from Point A to Point B, when suddenly he "fell into" a trial and "fell among" thieves.

Trials are not punishments from God, and they are not consequences of sin (although sin can lead to trials or make a situation worse). This unsuspecting man fell into his trying situation. He stumbled into it. He didn't earn it, and he didn't deserve it. He didn't plan it, he didn't want it, and he didn't pray for it. He wasn't crazy, and he wasn't a masochist. He wasn't a fool or a martyr. He didn't anticipate it or see it coming. If he had, he surely would have gone another way or done whatever he could to avoid it. No, his trial simply presented itself. He came around a corner... and there it was.

Like this innocent man, the trials we fall into and encounter are external. They are not a result of sin. They are a surprise, a shock. They are unexpected and unplanned and undeserved. And there is never, never a good time to fall into a trial.

Trials are also turning points. Corrie ten Boom wrote: "The turning point may be announced by the ring of the telephone or a knock on the door." In her own case she fell into years of trials as a result of a knock on her door by German soldiers. That knock was the turning point for her from a normal life to life in a concentration camp.

Corrie ten Boom fell into a trial. The poor traveler on the road through Samaria fell into a trial. And Tim Hansel fell into a trial. Each met a turning point. And I'm sure each expressed or thought something similar to these words written by Mr. Hansel when he learned his back was broken: "The life I'd always known was never to be again."

Obviously these examples are extreme. Some trials are large, life-shattering, and long lasting. Others, however, may only alter your day, your week, or the next month. For example, Corrie ten Boom mentioned "the ring of the telephone." We've all experienced phone calls that announce trials and signal that the life we've always known will never be the same. One friend told me about four separate phone calls she received over the years and the effects on her quality of life.

❧ Phone call Number One announced her mother-in-law was in the hospital. That call changed her day...or two. She canceled her commitments and off to the hospital she went to help her mom-in-law.

❧ Phone call Number Two announced her father needed bypass surgery. That call changed several weeks of her life as she canceled everything, called airlines, booked a flight, and left that afternoon to help her mom and dad.

❧ Phone call Number Three announced that her teenager was in a car wreck. Her son was fine, but that call changed the family's financial condition immediately and for the next four years as they forked out money for auto repairs and the increased auto insurance rate for their teen.

❧ Phone call Number Four announced she had cancer. As you can imagine, that phone call changed her day and all her tomorrows. Yes, that phone call changed her life forever.

You've encountered various trials, faced a turning point or two or more, and responded to rings from your phone. So have I. You know too well about the variety of messengers that can make it clear you've fallen into a trial. But now you know what your next step is to be: You are to count it all joy when you fall into or encounter trouble.

Experiencing a Variety of Trials

Variety is the spice of life. Well, perhaps variety is also the spice of trials. James' second word to us on discovering the solution to trials is to realize that we will "fall into *various* trials." Trials come in every sort, every size, and every intensity. We could also say we will "fall into *many* trials," many kinds and many times.

The means of our trials vary as well, which emphasizes not the number but the diversity. They are never alike. Trials are not the same for any two people. They are like snowflakes, each unique and different. This means you can't compare your life situations, or your husband's, or your children's to anyone else's.

> *Trials are not the same for any two people. Trials are like snowflakes, each unique and different.*

For instance, when my Jim was an army reservist during the Persian Gulf War, he was put in charge of processing the men and women who were going to the Gulf. He was also to assist their families with everything from their finances to their emotions. Some soldiers received phone calls that meant they deployed on the next plane. That was a tough trial they and their families had to deal with.

But my trial was different. The army put Jim on alert and told him to put his duffle bag by the front door and wait…and wait… and wait some more. For five months we waited for a phone call that would send Jim to the Persian Gulf. In the process I told Jim, "I know how to deal with you going. As soon as we were married, you had to go for six months of army training. And you go on so many mission trips that I have learned how to get by during your absences. But it's hard for me to endure this waiting for the phone to ring." Waiting was the test God had for me, and for me it was the harder test. For other wives, perhaps the harder situation was to have their husbands actually gone.

Here's another example. I know two separate wives who have lost their husbands. For one, her husband's death was instant. It came without any foreknowledge or warning. He drove out of their driveway to go on a business trip. She casually waved goodbye to him, still in her robe, coffee cup in hand...and she never saw him alive again. For her, it was the ring of the telephone later that night that caused her to fall into her trial, giving her the news of her mate's death.

My other friend's husband was born with a congenital disease. He knew all his life that it would be a short one. When he married my friend, they both knew they were on borrowed time. In fact, God gave them ten years over what doctors had predicted his lifespan would be. God gave them time to have a family and raise their children. When the husband and dad began to degenerate, he had time in the hospital—time to talk to his wife, time to give her leadership advice and words of direction and comfort and love to cling to in the future. He had time to talk to each child, express his love, and exhort them to live as passionate Christians.

These two noble women's situations show us the meaning of James' reference to the variety of hardships. Each lost a husband, but there was a difference in the circumstances they walked into and through. One couple lived each day with a death shadow over them. The other couple didn't have a clue. There was variety in intensity during their trials, varieties of length of time involved in their trials, and varieties of duration and results of those trials.

— Taking a Step Forward —

As you fall into and face your various trials—also known as bumps, roadblocks, and dead ends!—let these truths or steps guide you down God's path.

Step 1: Be sure what you are encountering is not the result of some sin, shortcoming, or wrong choice on your part. There is never a place for joy when sin on your part is involved. Be quick to confess any acts of disobedience to God if that is the case and then move on.

Step 2: Refuse to compare your trial or your suffering or your life with anyone else's. That is a principle taught in the Scriptures:

- 🦋 You are not to compare yourself or your dilemma with your peers. To do so is not wise (2 Corinthians 10:12).

- 🦋 You are God's workmanship (Ephesians 2:10). Don't compare how God chooses to work in your life with His methods and means for others.

- 🦋 You have been saved and called by God according to His own purpose (2 Timothy 1:9). Your trials help lead you to His purpose.

- 🦋 You can find joy and take pleasure in all kinds of trials. Second Corinthians 12:10 speaks of at least five different varieties of suffering.

- 🦋 You can do all things through Christ (Philippians 4:13). That includes counting your trials as joy and making it through them.

Step 3: Look to God for His joy and enablement as you walk on His path through your trials. Pray too for a genuine desire to adhere to His simple instruction to "count it all joy." You'll see remarkable growth in your spiritual life...and in your joy!

Step 4: Realize that God suffered. Jesus was beaten, buffeted, betrayed, humiliated, and murdered. Yet "for the *joy* that was set before Him [He] endured the cross, despising the shame" (Hebrews 12:2). Jesus knew the great joy that comes from accomplishing His Father's will. You too will know joy when you follow God without flinching and wavering, which pleases Him.

Step 5: Know that good can come out of your problems. Successfully enduring trials tests your faith and strengthens and matures you, causing you to be "perfect and complete, lacking nothing" (James 1:4).

Step 6: Don't forget to pray. You must pray, pray, pray about everything, at every moment, all the time—for your day and the unknown events that will come your way, for the phones and doorbells that are sure to ring!

Step 7: Look to the end results. Trials are not meant to defeat you. They are meant to be defeated. And trials are not meant to weaken you, but to make you stronger. When you have successfully navigated your way down God's path through each predicament, you will be stronger, more patient, and better able to cope with life and its demands. Joy will be yours as you walk with God on His path toward greater wisdom, faith, and usefulness.

Section 2

Becoming a Stable Woman

*Perseverance is not a passive submission to
circumstances—it is a strong and active response
to the difficult events of life. It is not passive endurance,
but the quality of standing on your feet
as you face the storms. It is not simply the attitude of
withstanding trials, but the ability to turn them into glory,
to overcome them.*[1]

5

Looking for Blessings

ぺ

Knowing that the testing of
your faith produces patience.

James 1:3

I hope you've been blessed to know several women who are very stable. You're never the same once you've met one. I'll never forget the first Christian woman I met who modeled stability. When I became a Christian at age 28, Jim and I began attending church. I got to know the wife of the teacher of our Sunday school group. She was so gracious and available. She took me under her wing in a mentoring relationship. Whenever I came home from meeting with her, I would tell Jim over and over again, "Oh, Jim, she's a rock. She's such a rock! No wonder her husband is such a man of strength. No wonder she has such an effective ministry to the women in our class. She's a rock we can all stand on, lean on, turn to, and depend on."

My new mentor was constant, steady, and secure. She and others like her have a powerful impact on all who cross their paths. They are towers of strength for you and me and provide a godly example of the kind of women God wants us to be. That's a goal God has for us—and that should be our goal too. We want to become stable women of God!

Life indeed is rich and full. There is so much to do as Christians to contribute to the people in our lives. And doing so requires us to be "steady as she goes." God tells us how this happens in James 1:3:

> *The testing of your faith*
> *produces patience.*

In other words, God uses trials to produce perseverance in you. Trials work patience into your character. They lead to steadfastness and develop endurance. They breed fortitude, causing you to become a stable woman.

Hearing God's Good News

As we continue learning more about how to navigate trying experiences God's way, His Word arrives with great encouragement. So far we've encountered a fact and a truth that initially tasted like bad news: We *will* have trials...*lots* of trials. And we will have a *variety* of trials. But now we receive God's good news...and more steps we can take to find His path through our trials. God gives us hope for our sore, bewildered, hurting hearts. Through James He delivers a promise: The testing of your faith produces "endurance" (NLT). Or put another way, the testing of your faith achieves staying power!

> *Staying power*
> *awaits us on*
> *the other side*
> *of our trials*
> *and testing.*

When I look at this one verse—only nine words long—and

break down God's good news, I see two bright, encouraging facts right away:

- ❧ This is the "testing" of my faith—not the breaking of it or the crushing of it.

- ❧ There is a prize waiting for me at the end of the testing process. It is the character quality of endurance. God promises that the outcome to any and all testing of my faith in Him will be positive.

Think about it. Attributes you and I greatly desire (and need!)—patience, endurance, and fortitude—are realized after we are tried. Staying power doesn't just happen. It's a result of the rigors and challenges of testing. Despite the seemingly negative process, there is a positive, life-changing message: Staying power awaits us on the other side of our trials and testing. That's what James says. We can know that the testing of our faith produces patience.

Sketching Out Staying Power

Exactly what is a stable woman, a woman with staying power? And how would you recognize her? She's one who endures whatever life brings her way. She doesn't crumble under pressure. She persists. For her there's no stopping allowed, no bailing out. There's no giving up and no giving in. And there are no excuses. She keeps on keeping on, staying to the end.

And that's not all. A stable woman is one who's steady. She's not soon shaken or easily rocked. Like my first mentor, she is a rock. She's constant, even-tempered, never fickle, and not wavering or fitful. She's steadfast and fixed. She's not a flake. She is faithful and solid.

As we think about this stunning (and rare!) trait, I'm sure that if you sat down to write lifetime goals, you would never dream of setting a goal to be a flake. You would never hope to become a quitter, or unfaithful, or weak. No, you would desire to be a woman faithful to the end—enduring, persistent, steadfast, constant. A solid Christian woman. In short, a rock. This hard-to-gain trait comes with an expensive price tag, for it is grown in the midst of turmoil. It is nurtured in pain and problems. It is cultivated in challenges and tribulation. As the statement at the beginning of this chapter tells us, stability and staying power possess the qualities of standing on your feet as you face the storms.

Looking to the End

I'm sure your days and weeks are a lot like mine—long and hard and full. Before my alarm even goes off in the morning, I know there is no way to get everything done...and that's if everything goes smoothly! But as you well know—and as James informs us—every day also has its startling deviations, its curve balls, its Plan B...and Plan C...and sometimes even Plan D! In short, its trials.

Two practices help me make it through each day. They also cause me to look for and find God's blessings strewn along my path. The first is focusing on the end. Fixing my eye beyond the work I'm doing in the present. Sure, I look forward to the end of every day and the comfort of my wonderful bed. But I also focus on the overarching end purposes for which I live each day—the goals I have to serve the Lord, serve my loved ones, and serve the people in my life. Those purposes make up the long-range view of my life and labors. They are the *reason* for all I do and dream of accomplishing. My desire is to bless others. I want to use my energies to make the best things happen. I am doing the best thing when I spend my time and strength on the best causes for the best end results.

The second habit that keeps me going through my days and my challenges is recalling at the end of each day all that was done and achieved. With my busy, full days—and the unannounced trials I faced—it is easy to berate myself for what was *not* done and forget to give thanks to God for what *was* done. With an eye on the day's blessings—instead of its failures—I clearly see God's grace, appreciate His enablement, recognize the wisdom He gave me along the way...and celebrate the triumphant joy of leaning on Him through the variety of trials I encountered. I recount the instances when God helped me in every difficulty I faced through the day.

Saints down through the corridors of time have looked to future rewards and blessings during their times of testing. In chapter 8 we will look closely at the men and women of faith on display in "God's Hall of Faith" found in Hebrews, chapter 11. Their perseverance in life bless and inspire me, and I know they'll do the same for you. For now, though, I want you to focus on the benefits *you* will experience as you look to the future—to the growth that awaits you on the other side of testing. Hear the heart of the apostle Paul, one who suffered greatly yet kept "reaching forward to those things which are ahead" (Philippians 3:13). Paul kept his heart and eyes fixed on "press[ing] toward the goal for the prize of the upward call of God in Christ Jesus" (verse 14). He wrote of gain on the other side of pain:

> *We learn how to calmly wait for God's help and the good that He promises will be revealed.*

- ❧ "We...glory in tribulations, knowing that tribulation produces perseverance; and perseverance, character; and character, hope" (Romans 5:3-4).

- ❧ "We know that all things work together for good to those who love God, to those who are the called according to His purpose" (Romans 8:28).

❧ "Our light affliction, which is but for a moment, is working for us a far more exceeding and eternal weight of glory, while we do not look at the things which are seen, but at the things which are not seen" (2 Corinthians 4:17-18).

God's message through Paul is easy to understand. He tells us suffering produces character. Through trials we gain staying power—perseverance. We learn quiet endurance, how to calmly wait for God's help and the good that He promises will be revealed. We become more stable as we trust in Him.

–Taking a Step Forward –

I love the writing and speaking ministry God has given me because I get to communicate with so many Christian women. It's almost impossible to manage all the emails, letters, and phone calls that come my way—a delightful burden to have. And I get to meet and talk with so many people during my travels to teach.

> God has already provided all you need to live this one day His way!

When I listen to dear women pour out their hearts—and their problems— I better understand James' reference to various trials and diverse kinds of suffering. My sisters in Christ are involved in problems that are physical, mental, social, economic, spiritual, as well as personal and family issues. Wow! Every woman has a variety of trials herself. Multiply that by the whole female population and you quickly realize the scope and variety of trials we run into!

What can you do to *stay* on God's path through your personal, multifaceted ordeals? Here are a few ideas:

Step 1: Face forward. Focus ahead. Refuse to look back... at yesterday's more carefree day...at last year's "best year ever" blessings...at other people's paths (which usually tend to look less rocky and demanding than yours). God has put *this* day in front of you, complete with its unique challenges. Furthermore, He has already provided—and will supply moment-by-moment, step-by-step—all you need to live this one day His way (2 Peter 1:2-4). God will be with you all the way.

What awaits you ahead? James says God promises patience and endurance, that precious and priceless staying power. Also God's "well done, good and faithful servant" will be waiting for you at the end of each day and at the sunset of your life.

Step 2: Focus on the positive. Watch the path carefully (you do have to *find* God's path and *walk* it), but don't forget to look up. Whatever challenges you encounter on God's path through your day, you have His help. Women tally up many things during a day, including carbs, calories, and checkbook totals. We watch our weight and keep track of how we use time (hopefully productively!). But the psalmist cautions us to "bless the LORD...and forget not all His benefits" (Psalm 103:2). At the end of each day recall God's goodness and count the many positive benefits you enjoyed.

Step 3: Focus on God's promises. James was thinking forward when he wrote, "Blessed is the man who endures temptation; for when he has been approved, he will receive the crown of life which the Lord has promised to those who love Him" (James 1:12). And Peter too was focusing forward when he encouraged his readers to think on promised blessings—the promised "inheritance incorruptible and undefiled and that does not fade away, reserved in heaven for you" (1 Peter 1:4). As a believer in Jesus Christ these promises—and many others—give you strength and comfort no matter what happens to you or what trials you must endure.

As you stay near to God on His path through trials, you can count on developing a deeper relationship with Him. Just as he promised, you will:

- ᛈ know His promised love

- ᛈ experience His promised care

- ᛈ partake of His promised provision

- ᛈ receive His promised wisdom

- ᛈ bask in His promised grace

- ᛈ behold Him face-to-face at your journey's end

Step 4: Face your trials knowing God is with you. Not only is God sovereign in all that touches your life—including trials—but He is with you every step along the path of your trials. He will help you through each difficulty you face. When you pass through the waters and walk through the fire He will be with you (Isaiah 43:2). When you walk through the valley of the shadow of death, He will be with you (Psalm 23:4). Like the dome of a great cathedral that softens and sweetens every musical note and noise, so God's providence softens and sweetens any and every affliction, grief, loss, and trial you encounter. His strength is available to you, empowering you and enabling you to stand on your feet as you face the storms. He will help you overcome your burdens and turn them into glory.

*If we cannot believe God
when circumstances seem to be against us,
we do not believe Him at all.*

Charles H. Spurgeon

6

Changing Your Perspective

ӿ

*Knowing that the testing of your faith
produces endurance.*

James 1:3 NASB

ӿ Recently Jim and I went auto shopping (due to recurring "trials" with an older car). During the outing we test drove a new car, and the salesman had us each drive it. When it was my turn, the man instructed me to go onto the freeway. After a few minutes in the slow lane, he yelled out, "Come on! You're babying this car. You're driving like a little granny. Put the pedal to the metal and see what this car can do!" It was clear he wanted me to *really* test the car, to push it, to go beyond normal driving. Maybe you've had this same experience.

Or maybe you've bought an article of clothing and noticed a paper inspection sticker with a number or name stuck on the material. That sticker means your garment passed the scrutiny of quality control. It was tested, it was tried, it was examined, and it passed.

Or perhaps you've seen commercials featuring the "Fruit-of-the-Loom Demolition Crew"—men and women allegedly hired to mangle and stretch articles of clothing bearing that brand name. These people (usually dressed in costumes representing different kinds of fruit) are intensely putting the undergarments through rigorous mauling because their job is to test them, to prove they are first-rate quality before they are put on the market for sale and use.

These examples give us the flavor of James' wording regarding the testing of our faith. He writes that *"the testing of your faith produces patience"* (James 1:3). Like my auto drive and the examining and testing of clothing or other items to ensure merchandise is bona fide and resilient, our testing and trials are designed to reveal proof that our faith is real, that it is indeed genuine.

Standing Up Under Pressure

"The testing of your faith produces endurance." Trials that come from the outside are the tests God uses to develop patience, endurance, and staying power within us. The Number One mark of a stable woman is that she has been tested and approved in numerous areas of her life and faith. She has repeatedly stood up under the pressures and trials. She has passed multiple tests. She's the real thing!

As we've already discussed, our spiritual testing—the testing of our faith—is meant to reveal the strength of our faith in God. The tests are not meant to break us. Nor are they meant to weaken us. The tests are applied because of God's knowledge that we *can* stand up under them. He knows we can handle the pressure…or that we must learn to trust Him and call upon Him to help us handle the pressure. He also knows that if we don't pass the test this time, eventually, with repeated opportunities, we will be able to hold up under the tests we initially failed. Therefore He applies tests again and again, sometimes using different circumstances, until we pass so we too know we can stand up under pressure. For example:

⊁ Samson failed repeatedly in his role as God's judge and leader of the people, choosing instead to fulfill his own selfish and sinful desires. But at the end of his life he passed God's final test. He gave himself unselfishly and died for God's purposes and His people.

⊁ Peter failed to stand up under pressure and denied Christ when questioned by a lowly, unknown maidservant. Yet later Peter stood up to the most powerful Jewish leaders on behalf of Christ, becoming all that Jesus' name for him meant— "Peter, the rock." And according to tradition, Peter died a martyr's death because he wouldn't budge in his faith in Christ.

⊁ John Mark failed miserably when he folded under pressure at the first hint of persecution and abandoned Paul's missionary team. But years later, after time and trials had matured John Mark, Paul asked him to come and tend to him and assist him while he was in prison. John Mark had become useful for Paul in ministry (2 Timothy 4:11).

Remaining Strong Through Affliction

At one time I belonged to a book group at our church that met once a month. We mainly read biographies of Christians. One of those books, now out of print, was entitled *The Persecutors*. It described the acts of a special squadron of Russian soldiers assigned to harass and torture believers in Christ. Yet the oppressed Christians never wavered in their faith. They remained steady and firm—patient!—as they trusted God through otherwise unbearable suffering and maltreatment and even death. Those who inflicted misery upon these saints could only come to one conclusion: There was absolutely no reason these tortured people could stand up under such treatment...unless God was real and His Son truly provided salvation and forgiveness of sins. As a result of witnessing their faith, many of the persecutors believed God would even provide salvation and forgiveness for sins as gross as the ones they, the torture squad, had committed. These Russian police became Christians.

Talk about trials! Everyone in the reading group was sobered and humbled and in awe of these faithful believers as their commitment to Christ and trust in God remained strong, empowering them to endure horrific treatment. One woman, after reading this disturbing book about the faith and faith-enabling courage of these Russian Christians, said, "Oh, I hope I can stand the test if something like that ever happens to me. I hope my faith is strong and real if that ever happens to me."

> *As you face each day, it's important to know your faith and trust in God are genuine. True faith will carry you through every difficulty.*

We also read the biographies of Corrie ten Boom, Jim and Elisabeth Elliot, John and Betty Stam, Helen Roseveare, Madame Jeanne Marie Guyon, and William Carey. A common denominator threaded throughout all these inspiring lives was the suffering, persecution, pain, torture, deprivations, losses, and deaths these saints endured that were all brought about because of their belief in Jesus Christ, because they were people of faith.

And guess what? After each book discussion, the same woman in our book club remarked, "Oh, I hope I can stand the test if something like that ever happens to me. I hope my faith is strong and real if that ever happens to me." It was obviously difficult for her to imagine herself in those kinds of trying situations, and the prayer of her heart was that her faith would stand up under such pressure. I believe she was honest enough to verbalize what the rest of us were thinking!

As you face each day and its trouble, it is important for you to know your faith and trust in God is real. It is genuine. Real faith will carry you through every difficulty that confronts you on your life journey. British pastor Charles H. Spurgeon noted, "If we cannot believe God when circumstances seem to be against us, we do not believe Him at all."

Defining Faith

So far we know that testing will occur (James 1:2 and 3). We also know that testing reaps benefits, producing patience or endurance (verse 3). Now we must pay attention as James teaches us something else. He tells us what is being tested—our *faith* (also verse 3).

What is faith? Volumes have been written to answer this question. However, the short answer is that faith is belief or trust.

Expanding on the short answer, faith is confidence in God and obedience to Him.

More specifically, faith—*genuine saving faith*—is belief in the Lord Jesus Christ that leads a person to submit completely to the authority of Christ and to put complete and exclusive trust in Him for salvation—for the forgiveness of sin and for the assurance and glory of eternal life.

Saving faith in Christ then leads us to daily, practical *acts* of faith and submission in all areas of life to the truths that God has revealed in the Bible.

Proving Your Faith

Let's look at what is *not* being tested. Your body is not being tested, although it may be involved in the process. One of God's servants, the apostle Paul, suffered from "a thorn in the flesh" (2 Corinthians 12:7). Yet after praying to God three times asking Him to remove this affliction, Paul rejoiced that God's grace was indeed sufficient and gloried in that truth. Nothing had changed. The "thorn" was still there, but Paul's faith took deeper root.

Your emotions are not being tested either, although your trials may bring them to the foreground, and you may even feel you are near a breaking point. Enduring ill-treatment, watching a loved one suffer or die, living under the same roof with an uncommunicative teen, sharing your life with an alcoholic husband—these and numerous other trials evoke strong emotions. The Bible calls Christians to control emotions, to walk through trials with *self-control* (Galatians 5:23).

So what is being tried? What is being proved? It is your faith. Faith is constant when circumstances are good. But when times are adverse your faith in God is exercised and surges. As the saying goes, "Adversity is God's university." It is His teaching tool. And tested faith results in tested character. Testing increases your ability to endure physical suffering. It teaches you how to use your mind to think and view life and its difficulties through God's eyes, through His perspective, which will almost always be vastly different from yours. He declares, "My thoughts are not your thoughts, nor are your ways My ways" (Isaiah 55:8). As you gain steady self-control and operate your life from the rock of faith your wild emotions will be tamed.

Rocklike character is the hallmark of a stable woman. And there aren't any shortcuts to achieving this. Hard-won character isn't just given to us at salvation. And it isn't earned by our deeds or by the number of years we've believed in Christ. It isn't bought or bestowed upon us. Character has nothing to do with our bodies... or emotions...or even the mind. No, it is tested and proven faith that makes its way through and endures difficulties that produces outstanding character.

Others Whose Faith Was Tested

If you have read any of my other books, you know that one of my passions is studying women in the Bible. It may be so interesting to me because I didn't have a Christian background or become a Christian until age 28. At that time I had been married eight years and had two daughters—a one year old and a two year old. When you've lived that many years with little or no exposure to the Bible, to its wisdom and teachings and the knowledge of Jesus Christ, life gets pretty hopeless. Almost every day is filled with failure. There are no solid principles or rules for living your life…or making decisions…or being a good wife and/or mother.

But on the day I was introduced to the truths about Christ— that He was the Son of God, that He died for the sins of people, that I could (by His grace!) receive Him as Savior, that I could be born again, receive forgiveness for all my sins, have new life, a fresh start, and partake of God's promise of eternal life—I immediately began to consume God's Word in the tiny Bible I found in our library. As I read God's Book I began meeting the many magnificent women in the Bible.

Note these examples of faith, of belief and trust in God. These women faced difficulties galore on their journeys through life. Yet they clung to God, trusted in Him, and walked with Him through their trials. They discovered God's help for every difficulty they encountered.

> ❧ *Noah's wife* was one of only eight people who believed and obeyed God. When God said, "Come into the ark" (Genesis 7:1), Noah, his wife, and their extended family rode out the worst flood the earth has ever experienced.

> ❧ *Rebekah* told her father "I will go" when Abraham's servant asked her to accompany him back

to Abraham's house so she could marry Isaac, sight unseen (Genesis 24:58).

❦ *Miriam* followed her brother Moses, leading the women onto the dry land that miraculously appeared when the Red Sea parted. She didn't fear for her life, but believed that safety and a better life awaited her on the path through the waters that stood back like walls on the right and on the left (Exodus 14:21-22).

❦ *Ruth* left all she knew to go with her mother-in-law Naomi to an unknown land because she wanted Naomi's God, the one true God, to be her God (Ruth 1:16).

❦ *The widow of Zarephath* gave her last handful of food to feed God's prophet Elijah, trusting in Elijah's God (1 Kings 17:12-15).

❦ *Esther* trusted God for her future when she risked her life to save her people, declaring, "If I perish, I perish" (Esther 4:16).

❦ *Elizabeth* found joy in her Lord...even though she suffered daily for many decades from the stigma and heartache of having no children (Luke 1:7).

I never tire of these women. How could I? They are true examples of real faith. They are role models for those like me who had none. And they are ever available to us. We only have to pick up our cherished Bibles and visit with them. Each of these women was tested—in ordinary and extraordinary ways. Each of them endured hardships like a good "soldier of Jesus Christ" (2 Timothy 2:3). And yes, they also fell, failed, and flailed. But they each went on—a true mark of genuine faith and a distinctive feature of a stable woman. They kept on going. They kept on believing. They kept on trusting in God Almighty, finally tasting the fruit of their faith, becoming partakers of heavenly knowledge.

—*Taking a Step Forward* —

How spiritually healthy is your perspective on your trials? And are any changes in your perspective overdue? Most people view "testing" as a bad thing. You probably dreaded taking tests in school. (I did!) You disliked having to take a driving test as a teen or when you moved to a new state. You feared the tests they administered when you applied for a new job. You probably passed some tests and failed others. (Okay, I'll admit that I had to take the Washington State driving test twice before I passed. I wish you could see my huge smile on my driver's license, which was taken minutes after I finally passed!)

But look at yourself now! Here you are today—a much stronger, wiser, mature, and stable woman. You are smarter, more seasoned, and more useful for having survived...and even excelled...in many of those tests.

> *God knows that trials will be for your ultimate good, that they will contribute to His purposes, and that they will bring Him great glory.*

Hopefully you see by now that testing is a good thing. It produces positive effects in your life. So why do we get so upset by the tests that come our way? Well, they aren't very fun, are they? We get caught up in the pain, anguish, or bother of the moment. Instead, we need to see them as God's way of making us better, more stable women, wives, mothers, daughters, grandmothers, employees, and church workers.

Just as you weren't sure why the teacher asked some of the questions on a science or history test, the teacher knew the reason for the questions—each one of them. And likewise, you may not understand why you're being tested in a certain way: But God does. He knows that it will be for your ultimate good, that it will contribute to His purposes and bring Him great glory as you pass each test and become more dependable and useful to Him. Then He can work through you even more to reach people with the Good News and accomplish His will.

Be encouraged as you step forward along God's path through your present and future trials. Be encouraged as you better understand the process and purpose of God's testing process. And be encouraged as you take in the wisdom of the bumper sticker that reads: "Please be patient. God is not finished with me yet!"

*The effect of testing rightly borne
is strength to bear still more and
to conquer in still harder battles.*[1]

7

Strengthening Your Staying Power

⅔

*You know that the testing of
your faith develops perseverance.*
James 1:3 NIV

When Jim and I first married, we lived on a honeymooner's budget, which means we did most of our furniture shopping at the local flea market. One day we discovered a wonderful antique brass bed. Orangey and almost black from the oxidation of the metal, its dismantled pieces leaned against the wall of a dingy booth behind other sparkling, more desirable items. But the price was right for us.

That old bed instantly became a treasure to us. But it had to be cleaned before we could use it and be proud of it. So we hauled our find home, set it up, and Jim went to work on it to see what he could do about the discolorization. When I checked on his progress later, I was alarmed that Jim hadn't taken a soft cloth and polish to the brass bed. No, he was laboring away with steel wool and caustic cleaner! And he rubbed…and rubbed…and rubbed. And the harder he rubbed, the brighter the brass shone. It came alive and was even more outstanding than we'd dreamed!

God's testing of us through trials has a similar effect on our faith in Him. His trials are good for us. They bring out the best in us. They prove what we are made of and what we've learned—or not learned—as Christians. They reveal how we've grown—or not grown. These tests are our vigorous "rubbing" by God. So we need to see God's involvement in our lives, as hard or difficult as it may be at the time, as a positive. That is possible because His tests contribute to us becoming stable—rocklike in character, solid and true, able to endure whatever comes our way.

Yes, oftentimes we don't understand the reasons for the tests and what they accomplish. We perceive them as negative and painful. But let's remember that old brass bed…and how it shone after some muscle work. Let's welcome the tests God sends our way. That way we'll shine as trophies of His grace!

Growing in Patience

Do you ever wonder "What's in this for me?" when you're going through a stretching time? James carried in his heart the suffering Christians to whom he is writing. In his straightforward way, he dove right into his message and addressed their trials head-on. But he didn't stop there. He next turned his focus on the positive results—what was in it for those enduring distress. James reminds and encourages his readers (and us!) that "the testing of your faith *produces patience*" (James 1:3).

What do you think of when you hear the word *patience?* Having to bite your tongue to wait for someone to finish speaking? Counting to ten so you hold off on blasting someone? These aren't bad coping mechanisms, but they don't represent the kind of patience James speaks of. He refers to something far grander—

endurance, steadfastness, and fortitude. My favorite translation of *patience* is "staying power."[2]

Think what patience and staying power would mean in your daily life. You would have the stability you need. You would have greater endurance so you would be less sporadic, less impulsive, and more dependable. Why? Because you stayed in the tests God gave you. You were tried...and found true. You were tested...and endured. You grew and now know you can hold up under adversity. You have more confidence and less fear.

Patience. This is a word for "abiding under" or for "staying"— persevering under or living under the pressure of the test while staying close to Christ. It means dwelling with Him whether it's in a den of lions (like Daniel—book of Daniel, chapter 6), in a fire (like Daniel's three friends—book of Daniel, chapter 3), in a ship at sea during a killer storm (like Paul—book of Acts, chapter 27), or in the trials you currently face. In any trial, it is you and God going through it. And patience and staying power grow because you hang in there! You see it through. You stay there until the testing is done. You stay until it's over. Now that's stability!

Once again, this is God's good news/bad news. The bad news is the reality and certainty of trials—all the trauma, the testing, the nuisances, the trouble, the pain, the tribulation. But hallelujah! The good news is that enduring through difficulties leads to greater trust in God—in His character and in His plan. That's a terrific harvest!

The Power of Rewards

Do you have a reward system for yourself? Do you ever say or think, "I can endure these next few hours...or months. I can make it through this doctor's appointment...this cancer treatment...this lab test...this meeting...this job interview or review. I can do this because something special is planned and waiting for me on the other side"? If you don't do this, try it. Rewards help!

When my husband wrote his master's thesis and I was doing

the typing—yes, on a typewriter—I kept telling myself, "I can do this. I can make this sacrifice. I can go through this because when it's finished Jim and I are taking a weekend vacation together." That's the way it works for me. I can better handle stressful times because there's something wonderful on the other side. There's a reward waiting.

And now I'm a writer...complete with publishing deadlines—bunches of them. Deadlines (meaning stress!) are part of my lifestyle. Every day before I even get out of bed the cloud of my next deadline rolls over me—even if the sun is shining (a rarity here in Washington State). Deadline stress is a problem for all writers.

But one day I listened to a CD made by an author who was solving this problem. He structured an entire reward system for writing and completing his books. He built in certain rewards all along the way—daily and weekly ones—and as his book deadline got closer, the rewards got bigger and bigger. He used the powerful motivation rewards provide for seeing something through.

Producing a Harvest of Virtues

Recall again James' statement: "The testing of your faith *produces* patience." *Produces* is a word used in agriculture to indicate a harvest or yield. For you and me, the harvest or product we gain from our trials is growth in faith and trust in God, along with the blossom of patience, which translates into staying power. Patience is a virtue that sees us through our problems and our daily lives. And blessings upon blessing, there are many more virtues—and rewards—harvested as a result of trials, including confidence, courage, constancy, and Christlikeness.

Confidence. Because of testing, I find when I get into a trying situation, I am able to think, *I've done this before. I've done this ten times before. I've done this a hundred times before. This is what I know to do...and I can do it again.* Or, as a speaker, I can walk onto a platform with confidence (although my heart is pounding, and I am praying with each step) and give a message. I know I can do it because I've done it over and over again. Yes, I rely on God—totally! But because He has faithfully and wisely taken me through this test multiple times to share His Word and wisdom with His women, there's staying power in me. And confidence comes with the staying power.

> *Battles yet to come are where courage is needed, courage forged in the fire of trials.*

Courage. As you face the trial at hand, courage comes from an experiential knowledge of God's presence. He's truly been with you all the way...through every trial to this point in time. You and He have done this before...again and again. And He will help you do it one more time. One gentleman got it when he observed, "The effect of testing rightly borne is strength to bear still more and to conquer still harder battles." Those battles yet to come are where courage is needed, courage forged in the fire of trials.

Constancy. To me this is an attitude or approach that thinks, *No matter what, I will become steady. No matter what!* For instance...

...what about pain? I once read a biography of Billy Graham's life and ministry. I learned that during one of his massive crusades, he slipped in a hotel bathtub and broke a rib. He went through the entire crusade preaching with a broken rib *and* without any painkillers! He refused all pain medication because he didn't want to take the chance of distorting God's Word in any way. He didn't want to be in a daze or a fog while delivering the powerful Word of God.

Pain is always a test. Pain asks of us, "Will you stay through the pain? Will you endure this to the other side? Will you be faithful?" Pain is only a test of your staying power. And you stay constant through pain by staying close to Christ…who "endured the cross" (Hebrews 12:2). Could Jesus have come down off the cross? Absolutely! But He stayed. He stayed there to do the Father's will. He stayed there to be the perfect sacrifice for sin so that people like you and me could have a relationship with God through Him. Like our Lord, we are to stay in our hard situations, in our trials, in our difficulties. We are to stay and stay and stay some more until the test is over.

…*what about tiredness?* A Harvard freshman came to the dean's office to explain why he was a little tardy in handing in his assignment. He said, "I'm sorry, sir, but I was not feeling very well." The dean responded, "Young man, please bear in mind that by far the greater part of the world's work is carried on by people who are not feeling well."

Tiredness is never an excuse. In fact, it's a test. If tiredness is our excuse, we have failed the test, and we'll have to go right back into the Refiner's fire (Zechariah 13:9). We must deal with this weakness. We must purge it from our lives. Stable women don't give in to tiredness. Instead they fight it. They remain constant and keep on keeping on…no matter what.

I will never forget one annual women's ministries kickoff meeting held at our church in the fall. We met on a Saturday morning in our church's gymnasium. At nine o'clock our pastor was to greet the women, bring a message of encouragement, and pray for our upcoming year of ministry. But guess what had occurred at the church Friday night? A time of all-night prayer and fasting. So at our meeting, when the woman making the announcements from the platform didn't spot our pastor, she said, "Well, I guess we're going to have to go to Plan B. I haven't seen our pastor.

He was probably tired and went home after our all-night prayer meeting."

Then out of the shadows in the corner by the back door our pastor, who had slipped in during her announcements, said, "I'm right here." After a sleepless night of leading our church in fasting and prayer, he had come to minister to us and bless us with a message. He made no excuses. He persevered. He hung in there fulfilling God's will!

Would tiredness have been an understandable reason for his not coming? Yes, of course. But not for this mature man of God. He didn't allow his lack of sleep to keep him from his commitment. Did he have staying power? Absolutely! He gave the church a full day of work. Then he stayed up all night at that prayer service. And the next morning he stayed at the church to deliver his message. He didn't let tiredness interfere with his commitments and purpose.

> *God isn't asking your heart to be in it. He's asking you to be there. To be faithful.*

...*what about illness?* Patient endurance means you come through even when you're sick. I have taught many times when I didn't feel well. I've gone to events and kept commitments when I was slightly ill. I've learned to follow through because I said I would. When I commit to speak somewhere, the women expect me to show up. On my part, I do everything I can do physically, medically, and practically to stay well. And in the past 20 years the only speaking engagement I've missed was one the weekend after the World Trade Center attack by terrorists in New York City on September 11, 2001. I was in Manhattan and air travel was frozen during those chaotic days, so I couldn't get to my engagement. My goals are to do my best to get where I say I'll be and do my best when I get there.

Sickness is a test. It asks, "Will you stay? Will you be faithful? Will you endure?" Staying close to Christ and abiding in Him takes us through the trial of illness.

...what about unhappiness? In my various ministries I've spent a lot of time with single college and career women. Wow, do emotions sometimes run high...especially when there has been a breakup with a boyfriend who also attends our church. The first thing many women say in this situation is, "I'm going to change fellowship groups. Then I won't have to face him. I just can't go in there and see his face."

Or, as one woman told me, "I just can't stand the pain. I'm going to change Bible studies." As her mentor I said, "Wait a minute! That's *your* Bible study. You were there before he was. You're going to let his presence keep you away from your Bible study?" I went on. "Those are your women there. That's your ministry. That's your Sunday school class." This woman decided to stay...and stay...until, in her words, one day she didn't feel the pain anymore. She had learned patient endurance.

Another woman I met with regularly echoed the same misery when she said, "I just can't stand to go to this ministry because he's there and I have to look at him." Again I said, "Well, this is your test for faithfulness." She replied, "But my heart isn't in the ministry anymore." I explained as gently as I could, "God isn't asking your heart to be in it. He's asking you to be there. To be faithful. We'll work on your heart being in it later, but now you need to get your body there."

I shared this counsel with these two women because we are to be "faithful in all things"...even when we're unhappy (1 Timothy 3:11). And that calls for staying power. Unhappiness, sorrow, and broken hearts are never pleasant. And they are tests. Will we persevere at our commitments? A stable woman, married or single, can't resign. She stays. Resignation is passive. It doesn't take or require anything to resign. Resignation is defeat. It's saying, "I quit." But perseverance and staying? These are active. Staying is a willful choice. Perseverance results in triumph.

In the end, the two women under my wing who experienced guy problems had victory because they stayed in their situations. They didn't resign or leave. God honored their determination to see their trials through to the end. He gave them the grace to patiently endure...until they grew...until their particular trials produced greater staying power in them. They were never the same after their testing: They were wiser, stronger, more stable, and rocklike.

Christlikeness. Do you remember my question "What's in this for me?" Well, here we stand at the ultimate benefit and reward of staying through testing to the end: We become more like Christ. Our faith provides the conditions for other virtues to grow. We are given an interesting command in 2 Peter 1:5-7:

> Giving all diligence, *add*
>
> *to your faith* virtue,
>
> to virtue knowledge,
>
> to knowledge self-control,
>
> to self-control perseverance,
>
> to perseverance godliness,
>
> to godliness brotherly kindness,
>
> and to brotherly kindness love.

In other words, a string of character qualities can and are to be added to or built on your faith in God and His Son. These qualities are to be a *chorus* or *production*. And faith is the starting point, the soil out of which these virtues are grown. Without faith we are no different than unbelievers. Both Peter and James knew believers have work to do. We are to give of our own efforts, "giving all diligence" in cooperation with God to produce the harvest of the characteristics listed by Peter. James reminds us that "faith by itself, if it does not have works, is dead" (James 2:17). As we faithfully add to our lifestyles virtues that mirror Christ's, others will witness His shining moral qualities reflected in us and be drawn to the Source—Jesus.

—Taking a Step Forward—

As we have journeyed this far on our quest to find God's path through our trials, have you noticed the beauty and strength of perseverance, of patience, of staying power? What is God asking you to stay in today? Is it a group or a job? Is it your marriage? Is it staying in a pregnancy when the world says you have an option? Is it staying alive and suffering when the world says you have an alternative?

There are almost always easy ways out of suffering and discomfort. But taking the easy way doesn't refine your character and produce endurance and patience. Nor does it honor and glorify our Lord. Each minute and each day as you step into a trial, remember that a stable woman stays and stays and stays. She stays through her breaking point. She stays through her falling-apart point. And then she stays some more. She discovers she is tried and she is true. She passes the test of genuine faith. She's the real thing!

The following three steps will help you stay on God's path through your lifetime of trials. They will give you God's help for every difficulty:

Step 1: Look to God. By faith believe that the grace and the aid needed in each trial will come from God. Know and believe that He will give you the strength to persevere. These provisions are blessings that come from Him alone. He will give you comfort in the midst of the trial and rescue you, whether in life or in death. Always look to God in trust.

Step 2: Look to Christ. He is "the author and finisher of our faith" (Hebrews 12:2). He left "an example, that you should follow His steps" (1 Peter 2:21). Jesus stayed. A sinless Jesus stayed in this sinful world until His work on earth was done. He stayed on the cross until His work of redemption of sinners was finished (John 19:30). He endured through the brutal, unjust treatment. He stayed on course through the jeering and taunting as people yelled at Him during His agony on the cross and wagged their heads in mockery of His painful movements. He stayed.

Like your Lord, you are to stay in your situation, in your trials and difficulties. Jesus will help you persevere and triumph. Always look to Him and His example.

Step 3: Look to the reward. God is your Master Refiner, and He values fire-tested faith (Zechariah 13:9). Trust in Him—in His wisdom, His plan, His purposes, His presence—when you are tested. Rejoice in His work and the harvest of virtues your trials will reap in you. Be glad that His purification process benefits others as you become more stable and provide strength and power to people in all situations. Be humbled that the resulting genuineness in you reflects His glory and brings praise and honor to Him.

Our greatest reward is the certainty of seeing Christ, of hearing His "well done, good and faithful servant" (Matthew 25:21), of receiving "the crown of life the Lord has promised to those who love Him" (James 1:12), of basking in the presence of God for eternity, enjoying "fullness of joy" and "pleasures forevermore" (Psalm 16:11). Look to the reward. As King David wrote, "I would have lost heart, unless I had believed that I would see the goodness of the Lord in the land of the living" (Psalm 27:13). Always set your gaze beyond your present pain and on to God's promised prizes!

Faith is not a hothouse plant that must be shielded from wind and rain, so delicate that it has to be protected, but [it's] like the sturdy oak which becomes stronger with every wind that blows upon it. An easy time weakens faith, while strong trials strengthen it.[1]

8

Standing with the Giants of Faith

❧

For when your faith is tested, your endurance has a chance to grow.

James 1:3 NLT

❧ Have you ever been on a vacation and stumbled onto a rare and unforgettable experience? Well, that's exactly what happened to Jim and me while we were celebrating our fortieth wedding anniversary in Paris. As we walked the palace grounds of Versailles on a warm, summer day, we wandered into a labyrinth of tall shrubs. We shuffled along for some time, not knowing how to get out of this vast garden...or knowing how we got in! Finally we strayed into a central passageway, a sort of shrine, where we found drinking water and a place to sit and cool off.

While we rested, we realized we were in a very special place... an outdoor gallery. As we looked around, we marveled at the myriad of larger-than-life marble statues that were strategically placed down a wide path that lead to a pond, which had a magnificent spouting fountain at its center. The statues framed by the green of the shrubs and the blue of the summer's clear sky created a beautiful scene.

Neither Jim nor I had any idea of the history behind the people represented by the many exquisitely carved statues. It was obvious though that every one of them was important, especially to the French. They were obviously revered and esteemed, and significant and famous enough for them to be remembered and honored as heroes through the centuries.

Marveling at Enduring Faith

Just as Jim and I experienced a rare treat as we sat and marveled at the beauty of our surroundings on that glorious day in France, we can look to, appreciate, and marvel at a group of men and women who were tested by the severest of measures...and triumphed. They believed in God, stood for a cause, and exhibited extreme courage in their individual circumstances. Yes, they stumbled at times, and yet their testing had positive effects as it confirmed and strengthened their faith. God recorded their stories in the Bible to stand forever as examples of faith and a source of great help to every believer. These heroic people are preserved for us in Hebrews, chapter 11, a portion of Scripture that has become known as "God's Hall of Faith."

As we take a brief look at these role models, focus on their perseverance, obedience, and faith. Remember *their* trials were God's means toward *His* ends and *His* purposes for *their* lives—the refining and strengthening of *their* faith. Also remember these people were flesh-and-blood, frail sinners just like you and me. But they are also examples of authentic faith and, because they were like us, we know we can respond like they did.

I have one more caution. Don't compare your personal difficulties with those of others—including the people mentioned in Hebrews 11. Instead, pay attention to how God helped these saints through the troubles they faced. He will do the same for you because "our God" is the same "forever and ever; He will be our guide even to death" (Psalm 48:14). Look beyond your trials to recognize how God will enable you to endure them, which will, in turn, produce greater faith in you.

God's Faithful Heroes

Enjoy these thumbnail sketches of the people God mentions in Hebrews 11. Follow along in your Bible, if you'd like. As you scrutinize each individual, appreciate the history of each one and his or her individual trials. Pay special attention to the evidence of faith in the lives of these men and women. You are in for a blessing!

Abel—the first martyr for truth. Abel and his brother Cain were commanded to bring a sacrifice to God, which became a test of obedience. You can read their stories in Genesis 4. Abel was confirmed in his faith and passed the test by offering the sacrifice prescribed by God and acceptable to Him. Cain, however, evidenced a deficiency of faith and a lack of respect for God and His command by making an offering that differed from God's instructions. In the end, jealousy consumed Cain and he murdered Abel. Abel's faith and obedience cost him his life. Cain could not accept or understand his failure or his brother's success and approval in God's eyes.

How about you? How are you doing in the Faith Department? Sometimes we fail to obey God's commands because they don't make sense to us. And sometimes we are less than willing to obey them for fear of unpleasant or harmful consequences. Don't fail the test of faith in God as Cain did. Be fully obedient to God. Your obedience will affirm your trust in Him and strengthen your faith as you rely upon Him. Believe (another mark of faith) that with God's gracious help you can endure any outcome or persecution from others.

Enoch—the man who pleased God. The brief glimpse God gives us of Enoch's life and faith is found in Genesis 5:21-25. Enoch lived during a time when the world was growing more wicked with each passing generation. So much so that God decided to destroy the world with a great flood. Enoch, however, didn't cave in to the wickedness of his day. He "walked with God" (verse 22). As a result of his faith in God and his intimate relationship with Him, Enoch didn't die. Instead he was taken alive to heaven.

Like Enoch, you and I live in a society that is growing more wicked with each passing day. We don't know how much pressure and persecution Enoch endured due to his faith and belief in God, but we can relate because we face similar problems as we walk with God today. Be strong in your faith! Don't let the world consume you or press you into its mold. Don't let anyone or anything knock you off God's path of faithful obedience. Follow Enoch's example. Make it your aim to be pleasing to God.

Noah—the man with a long-term commitment to obedience. God used Noah to prophesy and predict the coming of a great flood. The world had never seen anything like what the people of that time were hearing about. Mankind had never even experienced rain (Genesis 7)! Yet Noah believed God's warning and intentions and spent 120 years proclaiming the message of approaching doom and building an ark (Genesis 6:13–7:24). Can you imagine the ridicule and abuse Noah must have experienced during those years of building the first-ever boat in the middle of dry land and preaching about a coming judgment? As with his grandfather Enoch, Noah withstood the pressures of his time. By faith and through obedience he became an heir of righteousness. Noah's faith in God and His message saved him and his family, the only eight souls who survived the great flood.

Your trust in God will *always* make you different from those who do not believe in Him. You will experience rejection because you believe in God's Son, Jesus Christ, and in the promises of God. I believe that to Noah, God's command did not appear foolish. Noah believed what God told him. He left what was about to happen up to God as he faithfully went about doing whatever God asked...for however long it took...no matter what the cost. Noah seemed strange to his peers, but he, like his grandfather Enoch, found favor in God's eyes: Both walked with God during their lifetimes. As you confront your trials, lean on the Lord. Believe in His purposes and follow Him, no matter what. You can trust Him for the necessary endurance to carry out His will. That's faith!

Abraham—the man who surrendered all. Abraham was indeed a giant of true faith! You can find his story in Genesis 11–25. Abraham spent 100 years roaming the earth in surrender to God's command that he leave his home country and his kin. Consequently, Abraham was unable to permanently settle in one place or possess the land God had promised to him and his descendants. He also waited 25 years for the child God promised. Yet through all his wanderings and his anxious waiting for an heir, Abraham's faith and trust in God and His promises remained strong.

And Abraham's tests of faith didn't end there. Oh no! After his son Isaac was born, God tested Abraham's faith again, asking him for yet another surrender. God asked him to offer up his only son born of Sarah as a burnt offering (Genesis 22). Steady as a rock, Abraham took Isaac and left the next morning to do what God asked, trusting in God and His promises for him and his son. I'm sure Abraham prayed all the way to Mount Moriah while on the three-day journey to God's designated place for the sacrifice!

How did Abraham keep his faith going and growing during those difficult times? The Bible says he was looking at a future hope,

whether it was for the Promised Land or for the promised son...
even for the prospect of a resurrection if his son were killed.

Looking to God's promise of a future hope will keep your
faith strong too as you surrender by faith to God's design for your
life and wait for His deliverance in your present difficulty. How
patient is your faith? And how long can you endure your present
situation with an eye on the future? It may be years—perhaps
even 25 or more...or even a lifetime!—before you are delivered
from whatever trial you are experiencing now. But, like Abraham,
keep surrendering when your faith is tested. Keep trusting in a
loving and caring God whose perfect will is being worked out
with each passing day. Trust in God's timing, however long it may
take...even if nothing ever changes!

Sarah—"the mother of nations" and an ancestor of Jesus. What
a remarkable woman of faith! Sarah and her husband, Abraham,
were asked by God to leave their homeland and travel to a far
country...where they would never have a permanent home. (You
can read her life story alongside her
husband's in Genesis 12–23:2). And to
make matters more challenging, Sarah
was childless. Being barren in the culture
of her day was the worst trial that could
befall a woman. But God promised Sarah
a child—whose arrival took 25 years!
Sarah's faith was tested as she waited
through each passing day of each passing
year through the decades. For more than 9,000 nights Sarah went
to bed without a child...a child God had promised.

> *A faith that
> is tested and
> affirmed in
> difficulty is real
> and alive.*

Sarah, having long passed child-bearing age, was delighted
when God fulfilled His promise and gave her a son (Genesis
21:6). It was a miracle! Hebrews 11:11 tells us, "By faith Sarah
herself also received strength to conceive seed, and she bore a
child when she was past the age, because she judged Him faithful

who had promised." And blessing upon blessing, her son's lineage reached down through the centuries to the also-promised Messiah, Jesus Christ.

Are you about to give up hope? Don't waiver in your trust in the Lord. Look to Sarah's example for courage and faith to rely on God for one more day and night. Then get up tomorrow and trust Him again...and again...for as many "agains" as your test of faith requires. That's what faith is: Trusting in the unseen God for "things hoped for, the evidence of things not seen" (Hebrews 11:1).

Isaac, Jacob, and Joseph—three men who were blessed by their fathers concerning things to come (Hebrews 11:20-22). These three men represent three generations of fathers who gave blessings to their sons concerning the future. By faith each generation of men—who definitely had their share of troubles—believed in the promises of God and passed on their faith and hope as they gave benedictions to their children...who in turn trusted in those same promises. How sure were these men that God would fulfill His promise to give them a land of their own? So sure that Jacob and Joseph, while living in Egypt, asked that their bones be taken to Canaan for burial. They wanted to be buried at "home."

How viable is your faith in the future when you experience a trial? Is it strong enough to be seen by your children, family, friends, and workmates? Do you live out your faith and act upon it? Do you consider your faith important enough to be verbalized to your family members? A faith that cannot be seen and witnessed by others is questionable. James says, "Faith by itself, if it does not have works, is dead" (James 2:17). A faith that is tested and affirmed in difficulty is real and alive.

Moses—the "deliverer" God used to save His people. Moses (whose story begins in Exodus 2 and goes to the end of the book of Deuteronomy) was a man who had it all for a while. He was the adopted son of the Pharaoh of Egypt's daughter, raised in Pharaoh's house, and educated with the children of nobility. Yet he gave it all up and chose to identify with God's people. After defending a Hebrew slave, Moses escaped Egypt. Forty years later he suffered reproach and intimidation from the Egyptian Pharaoh when, as he again stood before this most powerful man in the world, he asked that God's people, the children of Israel, be allowed to leave. After many plagues sent by God through Moses, Pharaoh let the Israelites go. But Moses' troubles weren't over yet! He faced the wrath of the Pharaoh who tried to overtake Moses and the former slaves after they left Egypt. Furthermore, for many years Moses suffered the ongoing abuse, criticism, and constant murmuring of his own people as they resisted God's leadership through him, a path that led them all into the barren wilderness for 40 years of testing.

Moses truly suffered much for identifying with God's people. But the Bible says he suffered for the sake of the Messiah and God's suffering people (Hebrews 11:24-26). And the same is true for believers today. The apostle Paul wrote, "All who desire to live godly in Christ Jesus *will* suffer persecution" (2 Timothy 3:12). My friend, you are sure to suffer as you identify with Christ, who first suffered on your behalf. This should be reason enough to bear up under any difficulty—knowing you are suffering alongside your Savior and following in His footsteps.

Rahab—the prostitute who believed God was able to deliver. Rahab lived in Jericho, one of the most powerful city-states of her day. The people of the city had heard of God's miraculous judgments on the Egyptians and others who had dared to challenge God's people. Yet only one woman—a prostitute—responded in faith and fearlessly gave shelter to the Hebrew spies sent to check out the conditions in Jericho, an act of treason punishable by death. Rahab alone asked these men of Israel to save her and her family from the coming destruction. In the end, Rahab and her family were the only townspeople spared when the walls of Jericho came down (see Joshua 2–6).

Do you wonder what the difference was between Rahab and the rest of the people of Jericho? Two words give you the answer—God says it was "by faith" (Hebrews 11:31). Rahab was willing to give up everything, to turn her back on her country and her pagan gods, to even risk her life to follow the true God of the Israelites. By doing so she aided in accomplishing the purpose of God in Jericho.

> *Look to God for courage. Trust in Him. Believe in His ability to deliver you. Boldly travel through life and its trials with God as your ultimate Guide!*

What are you willing to risk, give up, and endure to follow the true God by faith? Look to God for courage. Trust in Him. Believe in His ability to deliver you. You can boldly travel through life and its trials with God as your ultimate Guide.

Saints of power and authority—men and women who led God's people. The people of faith cited in Hebrews 11:32 were warriors, kings, and prophets. Yet they are not praised by God for their positions, strengths, abilities, or nobility. Instead God recognizes them for what they accomplished by faith. Each one of them was courageous and, in turn, suffered great affliction because of obedient faith in God.

- ❧ *Gideon* went into battle against a massive army with only 300 men...and won.
- ❧ *Barak,* along with the prophetess Deborah, went to war and defeated the great general Sisera.
- ❧ *Samson* "shut the mouths of lions."

❧ *Jephthah* was empowered by God to defeat the people of Ammon.

❧ *David* lead the tiny nation of Israel as they "subdued kingdoms."

❧ *Samuel* anointed David as king and then evidenced his faith through a life of intercessory prayer.

Numerous nameless saints—people who courageously endured numerous trials. After going through a roll call of men and women of faith, the writer of Hebrews turns to generalities. There are so many feats of trusting faith in the history of God's people that the writer can't name all who exhibited genuine faith (Hebrews 11:33-38). These nameless giants are listed by their acts of great faith. They were tortured, mocked and scourged, put in chains, imprisoned, stoned, sawn in two, tempted, and slain with the sword. They went without clothing, were destitute, afflicted, tormented, were homeless, and hid in dens and caves.

—Taking a Step Forward —

Hebrews 11, "God's Hall of Faith," is quite a list, isn't it? In fact it's staggering! And I'm sure you've also read other stories of those who were martyred for their faith—missionaries killed for preaching the gospel of Jesus Christ; Christians sent to Siberia during the days of Communism because of their faith in Christ, and so forth. As chapter 11 of Hebrews ends, the writer adds that each of the heroes mentioned suffered not for a temporal reward, but for "something better" (verse 40). They had faith and withstood extreme suffering by anticipating the ultimate fulfillment of the promise of the coming of Messiah.

Today, when trials and tribulations come—and come they

will!—your faith and your resolve should be even more pro-nounced because Messiah came in the form of Jesus. You have Jesus! And now you look forward to His return! What a glorious time that will be!

What can you trust Jesus for today? Right this minute, what challenge is standing in your path? Are the little ones driving you crazy? Do you feel trapped? Useless? Remember, you walk with the giants of the faith.

Are you nursing your health…or a broken heart…or a loved one with cancer? Are you suffering unjustly because of slander or gossip? Are you going without a home, sufficient finances, a husband, or children? Remember, you walk with the giants of faith.

Realize that just as God was honored by the faith and fortitude of those incredible saints of old, He will be honored as you trust Him when you suffer.

No matter what God is asking of you, no matter what the size of it, ask Him to give you the grace to take even a small step of trusting obedience in whatever He requires of you. That one small step will put you on God's path through your trials. There you will experience His gracious help and provision, enabling you to stand alongside His giants of genuine faith in your times of testing.

Section 3

Becoming a Mature Woman

*Our trials are to cause us to rejoice and glory,
for we should realize that God is making us
weak that He may bestow upon us the power of
Christ! He would teach us not to glory in our own
insignificant, self-centered, sham vitality, but rather
in His Almighty, never-failing strength.*[1]

9

Crossing over to Greatness

ॐ

Let patience have its perfect work,
that you may be perfect and complete,
lacking nothing.

James 1:4

One of my ministries in the past was mentoring wives of seminary students. The hope our team of faculty wives had for these dear women was to see them grow in the Lord. We also wanted to provide some basic preparation for a broad base of ministry opportunities, to give the participants some experience before they went to their husbands' first ministries. Our goal was to equip these women to serve in some way in the place where God led them, whether it be a church, a mission field, or a Christian organization. What we offered was a three-year discipleship program for those who wanted the training. Many women from various backgrounds, levels of experience, and differing maturity came to the classes—some eagerly and some only because their husbands asked them to.

One year we "graduated" what I would term a "reluctant" seminary wife. Oh, she came to the meetings and classes, but she definitely left her heart somewhere else. She didn't really participate or contribute because she was clearly uninterested. When her spouse graduated they went to his new assignment. In one year they returned for a visit...and I received a phone call from her, asking to meet.

All I can say is that a very different woman came to meet with me! As we sat at my kitchen table, I was looking at a new woman, a humble woman, who now had a need to know. She was begging me, "Will you help me? Do you have anything you can give me? Can I get copies of all the handouts you gave out in our meetings? I'm sorry to say that I threw mine away." Then she told me, "It took the people in our new congregation less than one year to find out there was nothing to me. I was coasting on my husband's coattails. I had nothing to give."

As I once heard a seasoned pastor's wife say, "A congregation deserves a pastor's wife with *some* spiritual maturity." The average pastor's wife is probably not going to be the spiritual giant and leader her husband is, but there should be *some* maturity. When the wife uninterested in our class the previous year left by her husband's side, she looked good and could say all the right words. But when the people in her new church got close to her, deep down inside there was little or nothing of substance. I thank God that He worked in her heart to generate a desire to grow and serve Him and His people in greater ways.

Looking into a Mirror

God's plan for us as His children involves usefulness, which requires growth and maturity, which occurs as a result of trials and testing. No one desires to be immature, unable to handle new challenges, and ill-equipped to be of use to others. And we may not look forward to the trials that crop up along our way. But how else will we learn to stay in our trials and yield to God's instructions and plans for our growth? Realizing trials will come, accepting them with a joyful attitude, seeing them through to the end, and letting God perfect us is what maturity is all about. This is how and where maturity and usefulness is nurtured and grown.

James tells us trials will come. But he also tells us *how* to approach our tests and *how* to successfully endure them and reap the benefits God has laid up for us on the other side of the ordeals. James said to be "doers of the word, and not hearers only, deceiving yourselves. For if anyone is a hearer of the word and not a doer, he is like a man observing his natural face in a mirror; for he observes himself, goes away, and immediately forgets what kind of man he was" (James 1:22-23). So let's take a look into the mirror of God's instructions…and do something!

Moving Toward Greater Usefulness

Think about your life and its trials for a moment. As I reflect on mine I see it this way: I'm walking through life, going about the business of handling my responsibilities and lengthy to-do list (you know, like the one you have!). Then something happens. As I'm moving through my day, I come up against a trial. It appears out of nowhere. It isn't expected. There's no warning. I am merely walking along…and there it is. It's like suddenly coming up to the edge of a stream. There it is—right in front of me, blocking my progress. I can't move forward with my day—or my life—without crossing the stream, without crossing through this trial. So I have a choice to make. I can move backward to familiar territory, forfeiting forward progress, or I can dare to move right into the water, right into the trial. The latter is obviously the harder, riskier choice!

However, stepping into the water of this trial is the *right* choice because it's God's choice and His plan for my life. He wants me to move forward and onward to the other side and go on. He wants me to trust Him and grow. And what is on the other side of the stream? Of the trial? Victory. Growth. Maturity. Strength. Experience. Staying power. A greater contribution to God's purposes and His people.

Are you with me? Are you standing on the shore of a challenge? Well, good news! This is where the teachings from James 1, verses 2, 3, and 4, come to the rescue. They show the way to advanced growth and usefulness. The river's edge is where you are in your growth so far. As you stand on the bank looking at the water, realize you have to cross over to find the place of greater usefulness. And the only way over is by using the three stepping-stones God has situated in the water—three stones that reveal *His* path *through* your trial.

Stepping-stone #1—Approach each trial with joy. The first thing you have to do when you encounter any difficulty is to step into your test with joy in your heart. As James wrote, "Count it all joy when you fall into various trials" (James 1:2).

Stepping-stone #2—Be steadfast in the midst of each trial. "Knowing that the testing of your faith produces patience" enables you to make it through every problem to the greater usefulness and maturity that awaits you on the other side (James 1:3).

Stepping-stone #3—Cooperate with God's plan. Let each trial grow you spiritually. Learn the lessons God makes possible in hard or trying situations. His goal for you—His child!—is to complete you, mature you, and ensure you are fully developed.

James advises,

Let patience have its perfect work, that you may
be perfect and complete, lacking nothing
(James 1:4).

James is telling us in the form of another command "to let"—to allow—our staying power to achieve its work. He calls us to yield, to give place to something superior to our own comfort and place in life. A spiritually mature woman yields to her testing. She lets God and His trials do their work in her.

This personal yielding is similar to giving the right of way to someone else when we're driving. Every time my family drives to church we come to a yield right-of-way sign. We slow down and give way to pedestrians, bicycles, motorcycles, cars, and sometimes even an 18-wheel Mack truck! We yield right of way no matter how big or small the person or vehicle in our path. Why? Because the sign says to.

We also yield to those in authority over us. If the police come up behind us with lights flashing, we pull over. We stop. We yield to the police and follow their instructions.

In the same way James is telling us that as Christians we are to yield to God, to His testings of our faith, to His ways, and to His lessons. We are to "let patience have its perfect work." We are to fully cooperate with God as He builds our character.

Unfortunately, sometimes we do the opposite of *letting* or yielding. In fact, I've thought of at least seven ways we impede our spiritual growth and fail to grow up in the Lord. By identifying the ones that fit your tendencies you'll be better able to eliminate these hindrances.

Seven Ways to Fail God's Tests

1. *Resist.* Many times we find ourselves saying no to God. "No, I'm not going to do this. I'm not going to go through this. I'm not going there!" We fight and struggle against the test in front of us. But God is asking us to do the opposite, to "*let* patience have her perfect work," to yield to His perfecting activity in us.

I know you've been to the dentist, so you're familiar with

this scenario. You are helplessly lying in the dental chair. All the standard dental tools and paraphernalia are in and hanging out of your mouth. Before you realize what's happening, you've gradually closed…and closed…and closed your mouth until the dentist finally says, "Relax! Open up. Let me do my work. It will be less stressful and painful if you'll just relax."

> *We must trust God in every difficulty and every hard assignment. We need to do "the will of God from the heart."*

Our time and dealings with trials are like this. The woman growing spiritually yields to her testing. She relaxes her protective grip and fearful concerns. She *lets* her testing do its work. She submits to God and allows Him to accomplish His design. Then and only then will God's work *in* and *through* her be accomplished.

The Old Testament prophet Jonah shows us what it's like to resist God's will and God's work. Jonah's assignment was simple: Take a message of judgment to the people of Assyria in its capital of Nineveh. This assignment presented a real test for Jonah. He knew that because God was gracious and compassionate, He would show His mercy to these people who were enemies of Jonah's people (Jonah 4:2). Rather than submit to God's plan for his life as a prophet and God's gracious plan for the Assyrians, Jonah chose to resist. He fled from God (so he thought!) and from usefulness.

You probably know the story of Jonah and the whale. Jonah boarded a ship—one going in the opposite direction from Ninevah. While onboard resisting God's command, God used drastic means to bring Jonah around. The Lord arranged for Jonah to be swallowed by a great fish and spat out on shore…back toward Ninevah. He literally turned His prophet around so Jonah would cross his "river" and, in trust and obedience, preach God's message.

The result? Jonah was incredibly useful and instrumental in

causing thousands of residents of Nineveh to repent, thus escaping devastating judgment from God.

Like Jonah, we must trust God in every difficulty and every hard assignment. We must do "the will of God from the heart" (Ephesians 6:6). He will see us through and grow us spiritually in the process. Our obedience to step into, stay in, and see our trials through will produce a magnificent, finished piece of work. What God graciously accomplishes through us will ring His praises throughout the ages.

2. *Retreat.* Sometimes we fail to do God's will by retreating from our trials. We feel overcome by what we're up against. We're so fearful and overwhelmed that we go to bed…or take some pills…or call and cancel some things so we don't have to face people or responsibility.

Every test is a test of faithfulness. Sometimes all God is asking of us is to just show up! To get where we said we'd be. To keep the commitments we've made. To follow through. Instead we retreat. Take heart! We're learning how to move forward! A spiritually growing woman yields to her testing. Even with fear and trembling, she steps into the stream, setting aside her fears for faith and her trembling for trust. She faces her stretching challenges, trusting the God who is planting it in front of her, the God whose grace is truly sufficient to see her through whatever He asks of her. A woman who wants to grow in the Lord faithfully navigates the stepping-stones that lead her on God's path through her trials. She joyfully anticipates the promised endurance and maturity that awaits her.

"It is enough! Now, LORD, take my life." Does this sound like a man who confronted and defeated 850 false prophets on Mount Carmel? Elijah had stepped across many "rivers." He had trusted God on countless occasions and seen God use him to perform miracle after miracle. But now he was uttering words of discouragement and dejection (1 Kings 18–19).

So what happened to cause Elijah to disintegrate? He took his eyes off God and fixed his gaze on his latest trial—one woman, Queen Jezebel, and her threat on his life. How did God get Elijah out of his depression? He confronted Elijah with a need to return to his mission of serving Him. The Lord wanted Elijah to cross his next "river" and continue the maturing process He was working out in his life. Elijah needed to know that God wasn't finished with him yet. The prophet's ability to move forward was key to his future usefulness to God.

> *God is faithful and His timing is perfect. He knows what He is doing and how He will perfect us, strengthen us, and make us whole!*

Like Elijah, we grow weary. We become overwhelmed. Sometimes we can't see our way out of or through a difficulty. We think it would be better to be dead, gone, removed from the continuous suffering and heartache and harsh demands of life in this world. We think it would be better to give up rather than keep trying to go on, putting out the effort and energy our service to God and others requires. But God is faithful and His timing is perfect. He knows what He is doing and how He will perfect us, strengthen us, and make us whole—with nothing lacking!

Whatever you're facing today—and every day—remember God's promise: Be "confident of this very thing, that He who has begun a good work in you *will* complete it" (Philippians 1:6).

—Taking a Step Forward—

We'll move forward on our list of what we need to watch for so we don't fail God's tests in the next chapter. For now, pause and consider yourself.

Are you a learner or a yearner? Do you have a need to know and grow, or do you long to be somewhere else, to hurry up and get this day or this trial over with in any way possible? The young seminary student's wife yearned to not be sitting in the discipleship meetings for wives. But one year later she became a learner with a need to know. She eagerly desired help, strength, faith, and evidence of God's power at work in her life.

If you're a yearner at this point in your life and your spiritual growth—one who is waiting for something to end or get better—bite the bullet now. Look up. Pray. Tell God how you feel and why. Then ask Him for His ever-available help and ever-adequate grace to enable you to step into the river of your trial and move forward.

And if you are a learner, thank God for that attitude. And keep it fresh through prayer and continued trust in Him. You may also want to keep a journal of God's daily enablement and the lessons you learn to encourage and motivate you. The psalmist advised us to "never forget the good things he does" (Psalm 103:2 NLT).

> *No matter what the cost or the temporary pain of your trials, God promises maturity, usefulness, and a deeper knowledge of Him.*

Do you want what is on the other side of your trials? The list of blessings is endless. It includes:

- ❧ more Christlikeness
- ❧ spiritual growth
- ❧ greater knowledge of God
- ❧ deeper faith in Him
- ❧ strong, sterling character

- ❧ wisdom

- ❧ experience

- ❧ a heart to help others

Don't fail to take the next step in your adventure into God's purpose for *you* and His *use* of you! The apostle Paul put our present difficulties into perspective: "Our light affliction, which is but for a moment, is working for us a far more exceeding and eternal weight of glory" (2 Corinthians 4:17). No matter what the cost or the temporary pain of your trials, God promises maturity, usefulness, and a deeper knowledge of Him that can be used to help others. As Paul praised,

> Blessed be the God and Father of our Lord Jesus Christ, the Father of mercies and God of all comfort, who comforts us in all our tribulation, that we may be able to comfort those who are in any trouble, with the comfort with which we ourselves are comforted by God (2 Corinthians 1:3-4).

Do you desire greatness? God's blessings? Then take care to embrace and manage the tests that come your way. Step willingly into the river of each trial. Cross over to greatness in service to your Lord and to others.

Too many Christians are looking for an easy
way out of life. They think that if they had no burdens
they could live pleasantly and triumphantly.
They do not realize that God often keeps us up
spiritually by keeping us down physically. The weight
of trial gives our feet spiritual traction.[1]

10

Making Decisions that Develop Greatness

ᣔ

Let endurance have its perfect result,
so that you may be perfect and complete,
lacking in nothing.

James 1:4 NASB

"Greatness" in the world's eyes is power, rank, and fame. But greatness in God's eyes entails service and usefulness to Him and to others (Luke 22:26-27). That's what we considered in the previous chapter. To achieve God's greatness, we must first overcome our tendency to sidestep His trials.

What are some ways you and I miss God's lessons and don't grow spiritually? I promised you seven insights into how we avoid trials. These seven methods were all drawn, I'm sorry to say, from my own experiences. As you move ahead through more of the list, remember that we've already examined two of our pet ways of keeping ourselves out of the trials God sets before us: We *resist* and we *retreat*.

3. *Resent.* Instead of getting onboard and marching forward into the trial in front of us, we resent the roles others play in our difficulty. Although God is absolutely sovereign in our lives, we mistakenly think others have contributed to our coming to this particular place of pain and suffering. We can also be tempted to be irritated with God for subjecting us to this hardship. But God has a grand plan for our trials—each and every one of them. He wants them to help mature us and benefit His purposes.

Resentment is a growth killer. In fact, it moves us in the opposite direction of God's maturing process. It can lead to sinful actions and inhibit or prevent the positive character development God desires in us.

I remember standing beside Jim one morning at church while he visited with a man who said he had finally gotten a job after months of unemployment. He gushed, "I'm just praising God I have a job." He went on. "I don't get home until nine or ten o'clock at night, but I'll gladly see patrons at eight if that's when they want to come and pay me to work. Afterward I praise God no matter how late it is!"

While he was sharing his joy, I was thinking, *There's a wife in this story who is waiting for an absent or late husband and father at home. I hope she's accepting this trial with joyfulness…counting it all joy when her husband is late getting home at night because he has a job.*

It's easier to resent our husbands, our job or his job, our children and the trials having them brings each day (sometimes each minute!), or our singleness (and on and on the list of challenging life situations goes) than it is to face our trials head-on. It's easier to feel bitter about our in-laws, our parents, our bosses (and on and on the list of resentees goes) than to grow up and out of this immature practice. I'm sure whatever you can name, we find a way to blame it or them. But we must put annoying people and situations and resentments aside and look full into God's wonderful face. We need to trust Him and His will for us rather than resent those who present a problem to us.

When I minister to college-age young women, I find a really big problem for many of them is their parents. As I meet with the young women, I ask those who are caught in the trap of resenting their parents, "Who knew from before the foundation of the world who your parents would be?" Suddenly the light goes on as they realize they are resenting the parents God specifically gave to them, who will help bring about the development and maturity He has planned for their lives.

> *A spiritually mature woman realizes God is at work in her life through people—with all their quirks and irritations, with all their shortcomings and sinful behavior.*

Then a young woman gets married. And now she has in-laws. If she hasn't allowed her parental trials to teach her the valuable lesson of yielding to God rather than resenting others, she may add her new in-laws to her list of "People I Resent." But the parents of her new husband are now part of God's divine plan to bring about what He has in mind for her and her growth. They are God's instruments in her life. A spiritually mature woman realizes God is at work in her life *through* people—with all their quirks and irritations, with all their shortcomings and sinful behavior.

Sarah, Abraham's wife, is a sad illustration of sinful resentment. God had promised Abraham, an heir...yet Sarah remained childless (Genesis 16:1-6). What did she do? Sarah decided to help God fulfill His promise by using a common practice of the day and offer her servant, Hagar, as a substitute wife to her husband for the sole purpose of having a child. Sarah, at least for a time, failed to trust God to fulfill His promise through her. Sarah's scheme worked—but with disastrous consequences. The pregnant Hagar became haughty, which increased Sarah's resentment, which Sarah took out on her. In fact, her handling of her handmaiden was so harsh that the pregnant woman fled into the desert, wanting to die rather than be subjected to Sarah's cruelty.

Hagar, however, returned because an angel of the Lord asked her to. Soon Hagar's child was born, and Sarah's resentment smoldered even hotter toward her servant and grew to include the child...and even her own husband for his part in the scheme! Rather than trust God, stay in her trial, and wait on the Lord, Sarah tried to sidestep God's process. As a result she ended up bitter and mean toward those closest to her.

Now contrast Sarah with a spiritually mature woman who yields to her testing. She doesn't resent her tests or the people involved in them. And she doesn't blame those people either. She realizes God is at work in her life *through* these "sandpaper" people. She knows God has a goal in mind for her—that she become a whole person, steady under trials and trauma, and mature in every area of life, willing to wait for God to act on her behalf. She takes on the attitude of Job, expressed when his family and possessions were killed and destroyed, "The Lord gave, and the Lord has taken away; blessed be the name of the Lord" (Job 1:21).

Oh yes! I don't want to forget the best part of Sarah's story. It's found on the other side of Sarah's river of testing. Finally Sarah got it. She learned what only her 25-year trial of wondering and waiting could teach her: She grew to trust God. So much so that "by faith Sarah herself also received strength to conceive seed, and she bore a child when she was past the age, because she judged Him faithful who had promised" (Hebrews 11:11).

When life seems to be on hold, don't resent the people, events, or circumstances in your life. Stay in your trial. Stay joyful. Keep your mind and heart upon God! Let Him have His perfect work in you so that you will be a mature woman—strong in character and fully developed, perfect and complete, lacking nothing.

4. *Denial.* Have you ever denied that you had a shortcoming, a weak area, a flaw in your character? Have you failed at something but wouldn't admit it? Have you denied knowing someone for fear of persecution that might result from associating with that person? Maybe your reasoning goes like this: "A blind spot, you say? You think I have a sin area I'm not recognizing or admitting? Well, you're wrong. I don't have a blind spot. I don't have this flaw...or that weak area."

It's so easy to deny what we want to ignore. All we have to do is quickly put our mouth on autopilot and blurt out, "No, you're wrong." In a few swift words we deny that we need the lessons God wants us to learn, which means we fail to enter into the stream of testing. We choose instead to stay on the shore, stuck at our present level of development...or lack of it. We promptly, without prayer or contemplation, refuse to believe that God is sending us to His school to learn something that will complete and perfect and mature us.

That's what the apostle Peter, "the rock," did. And the amazing thing is that Jesus warned Peter of his weakness...and still Peter denied and failed. Here's what happened.

Jesus told Peter in straight language: "Satan has asked for you, that he may sift you as wheat. But I have prayed for you, that your faith should not fail; and when you have returned to Me, strengthen your brethren." And what did Peter say to this? "Lord, I am ready to go with You, both to prison and to death." To which Jesus replied, "I tell you, Peter, the rooster shall not crow this day before you will deny three times that you know Me" (Luke 22:31-34).

And that's not the end of Peter's testing and failures! Sure enough, Peter did deny his association with Jesus just as the Lord said he would. Why did Peter deny knowing Jesus? After all, the first time it was only a lowly maidservant who asked him if he knew Jesus. Why did Peter deny his close relationship with his Savior and Master? Take heed to this list of reasons drawn from Luke 22:45-60. They show us a definite drifting off God's path.

❧ Peter slept when he should have been praying (Matthew 26:40).

❧ Peter fought and cut off a soldier's ear when he should have heeded Jesus' cue and done nothing (John 18:8-11).

❧ Peter deserted Jesus at His arrest, and then followed Him from a distance (Matthew 26:55-56,58).

❧ Peter sat among the crowd while Jesus was accused instead of standing with and supporting Him (Matthew 26:58).

❧ Peter denied Christ instead of speaking up and owning the truth about his relationship with Jesus (John 18:16-17,25-27).

When others truthfully let you know of a shortcoming or warn you that a certain behavior is sure to bring uncomfortable results, quickly take these steps:

❧ *Stop* doing what you're doing.

❧ *Look* at your life and what God's Word or messenger is saying.

❧ *Listen* to what God has to say to you through prayer.

❧ *Correct* your ways.

Do you want to make decisions that develop greatness? Then make it your aim to choose the harder path—the profitable one!—and stay near to God. Don't do like Peter did and deny your faults and drift away. Admit your shortcomings, step into the water, face the trial you've been avoiding, and head for the other side—the side of growth and perfection. God will go with you all the way. He will help you triumph over your weakness.

5. *Comparison.* When we meet up with difficulties the temptation is to draw a comparison between our trials and those of others. We inaccurately say, "I'm the only one who has to go through this, to suffer this. No one but me is facing what I'm up against. No one else I know has this problem to this level."

Consider this scene involving the disciples Peter and John. Jesus questioned Peter's love three times in John 21, and then told Peter, " 'When you were younger, you girded yourself and walked where you wished; but when you are old, you will stretch out your hands, and another will gird you and carry you where you do not wish.' This He spoke, signifying by what death [Peter] would glorify God" (verses 18 and 19). Jesus was telling Peter he would die a painful death, but in his manner of death he would honor his commitment to Him.

> *The shortest way to maturity is God's path, which leads straight through our trials.*

And what did Peter do next? He turned around, looked at John, and asked the Lord, "But Lord, what about this man?" (verse 21). It's no wonder the Lord rebuked Peter, saying, "What is that to you? You follow Me" (verse 23).

Oh, are we ever like Peter! Our sinful nature naturally compares what we're enduring with someone else's life and his or her seeming lack of trials—or at least lesser ones, we are sure. We say, "But what about him? What about her? What about that family? What about that situation? What's happening to me didn't happen to them. They seem to have no problems at all. And just look at all my troubles and woes!"

But this comparison doesn't work. First of all, it's not wise (2 Corinthians 10:12). Another reason is because God works in His children's lives in different ways and through "various" trials (James 1:2). Paul mentions five different kinds of suffering in 2 Corinthians 12:9: infirmities, reproaches, needs, persecutions, and distresses. Also comparing ourselves, our suffering, our trials, our circumstances, with those of others indicates we are questioning God's wisdom and justice. Jesus basically says what happens to others isn't our business. Our business is to follow Him and keep our eyes on Him (John 21:22).

We all have miles to go on the road (or miles to swim in this river!) to spiritual maturity. The shortest way to maturity is God's path, which leads straight through our trials. To reach the growth He desires for us, we must yield to our testing without questioning His choice to allow it and refuse to compare ourselves to others. God is too wise to make a mistake and too loving to ask us to submit to trials without them being for our best good and His best plan. God has a special set of circumstances just for you that prepares you for even greater usefulness to Him.

Aren't you glad God lets us see the end results of His work in Peter's life? Peter eventually chose to step boldly into his unique trials of ministry. He chose to step forward into the river in front of him. He chose to stay in the trials until he reached the other side—to an amazing life of ministry and the ultimate joy of heaven, where there is no more suffering, tears, or death. Christian tradition indicates Peter suffered a painful death—death by crucifixion. But he requested to be crucified upside down because he felt unworthy to die in the manner his Lord had died. Peter did not deny Christ to avoid execution! Certain evidence of spiritual growth and maturity.

–*Taking a Step Forward* –

Did you note Peter's maturity? His path toward greater growth? What was the developmental process? Answer: Trials, trials, and more trials. He went through many failures before going the distance to the other side of his tests. But in time, as a result of this testing, he lived up to the name Jesus gave him: Peter, the rock. Once Peter learned not to deny his weaknesses—or his Lord—and not to compare his trials with that of others, his life took on the character of rock, of granite. He became unshakeable, unwavering, and a leader of leaders in the early church. Pray to follow in the mature Peter's steps—to make decisions that develop greatness—and step out on God's path through your trials and use the stepping-stones He has provided for your growth and perfection.

And remember Sarah too. Her trial was a long and trying ordeal. Imagine 25 years—not hours or weeks but years!—of wanting something you were promised and seeing no glimmer of the assured fulfillment. Yet Sarah stayed. She stayed with Abraham. She continued to follow her husband as he followed God and "went out, not knowing where he was going" (Hebrews 11:8). The way was rough, and definitely long, but her faith grew through the process. When Sarah conceived and delivered the promised son, everyone knew—including Sarah—what a miraculous thing God had done. Sarah had certainly tried doing things her own way, but God's way came about and He was greatly glorified.

And, dear reading friend, that's what our joyful acceptance of trials, along with our decision to stay in them, does. We mature and the results are praise and honor and glory to God! Our maturity and stability is humanly impossible to get on our own because they are of God. His doing, His plan, and His grace brought them to pass.

Let patience have its perfect work that you may be fully developed and perfectly equipped, complete and lacking nothing.

Become a tower of strength for God's sake. Be joyful when life is not joyful for God's sake. Be willing to grow to the point of utmost usefulness to God and others for His sake.

What step do you need to take this minute? Decide to accept your trials. Ask God for His help and seal your commitment with a prayer of thanksgiving for His lovingkindness, mercy, grace, and good plan for your life.

The things that hedge us in, the things that handicap us, the tests that we go through and the temptations that assail us...draw us closer to the Lord so that the testimony of our lives will count more for God...When we have limitations imposed upon us we do our best work for the Lord, for then we are most dependant on Him.[1]

11

Dealing with Roadblocks

❧

*Perseverance must finish its work
so that you may be mature and complete,
not lacking anything.*

James 1:4 NIV

Several years ago Jim and I made a major move, the first one in 16 years. You can imagine the disruption and chaos. Not only did we move from sunny Southern California to the soggy Pacific Northwest, but we also moved from the large home where we raised our family, flung wide the doors for Bible studies, housed guests, and hosted family and related activities for two weddings. And where did we resettle? In a unique, impractical, sort of cabin in the woods. It's perfect for the two of us, a family dinner, and an occasional visitor...as well as long days of writing.

This downsizing meant we had furniture and "stuff" galore... and no place to put it. For some time this "stuff" was placed in a storage unit while Jim and I continued to run hard to keep up with our fast-growing family (including grandkids!), our commitments, and our many responsibilities and ministry travels.

Finally the day arrived when we acknowledged we would never realize our dream of being truly organized and having our house in order until we dealt with the out-of-sight accumulation from our 35 years of marriage and family life. Jim and I dove into the storage unit. We sifted through it, made decisions about what to do with each item—whether to keep a box of files or knickknacks, a set of extra box springs and bedrails, a cherished-but-where-do-you-put-it trunk my dad made for me when I married, and so on. One by one, piece by piece, and day by day we cleaned out the majority of items that were keeping us from enjoying the order and freedom we craved.

In the same way that a temporary room full of unused, excess possessions robbed Jim and me of an unencumbered lifestyle and held us back from truly moving forward, so the list of reasons for not graciously accepting our trials we've been discussing holds us back. So far we've gone over: 1) *resist,* 2) *retreat,* 3) *resent,* 4) *denial,* and 5) *comparison.* When we fail to enter into our trials, we postpone a better life, greater growth, and the spiritual maturity we long for and God desires for us.

I trust you've been confronting some of these excuses and the pet ploys you pull out when faced with trials. How are you doing? I pray you are enjoying your transformation and realizing the blessings and benefits that staying in your trials harvest.

Now, let's move on. There are a few more common problem attitudes—roadblocks!—for us to consider...and deal with.

Dealing with Roadblocks to Progress

6. *Pride.* Generally we want others to think the best of us, don't we? We want to put our best foot forward. We want to have it all together...or at least appear to. We worry while we go through testing about what other people will think when they see us

struggling with this situation. We worry about what others will think when it becomes known what specific problems we're dealing with. We also get anxious about what we look like when we're suffering physically.

Our solution? Clam up and avoid contact with people. When we're suffering physically we withdraw and stay home until our appearance is improved. When we face certain trials we stop going to church or out in public, all the while telling ourselves we'll resume our interaction with others, our ministry commitments, and our attendance at worship *when* we look better or feel better or get over this or make it through that.

> *Let God use others to assist you as you make your way through your trial. This shows your maturity and lets God work through the other person.*

When it comes to dealing with pride and remaining humble and open, the apostle Paul is a positive role model for us. He wasn't too proud to allow others to help as he experienced his numerous trials. Paul wasn't self-sufficient. He didn't nurture a martyr complex or have a "poor me" attitude when he suffered.

- ❧ Paul allowed the church at Philippi to send help and money while he endured distress in prison (Philippians 4:15-18).

- ❧ In a letter to Timothy, Paul asked him to retrieve his cloak he had left at a friend's, get Mark, and come to Rome to help him during his last imprisonment (2 Timothy 4:9-13).

- ❧ Paul accepted the hospitality and friendship of Priscilla and Aquila. He stayed in their home and

worked alongside them as he stepped out in faith
to minister the gospel in Ephesus in the midst of
opposition. They even risked their lives for him
(Acts 18:2-3; Romans 16:3-4).

These are but a few examples of Paul's sufferings and his need
for the aid of others during harsh times and ministry trials. He
didn't worry or wonder about what others thought of him. In fact
he announced, Yes, I am in prison, but I am the Lord's prisoner
(2 Timothy 1:8)! And he revealed an attitude of humility when he
announced, "I am the least of the apostles, who am not worthy
to be called an apostle, because I persecuted the church of God.
But by the grace of God I am what I am, and His grace toward
me was not in vain" (1 Corinthians 15:9-10).

Like Paul, a woman dedicated to God—a woman who accepts
God's will, fully trusts in Him, and courageously steps into her
trials—is never too proud to connect to God *in* her trial and ask
for and accept help from others as she yields to her testing.

Please don't fall prey to pride. Look to God for *His* purpose,
His approval, *His* understanding, *His* companionship, and *His*
"well done" as you faithfully wade into the river. Don't worry what
others think or might think. Set your eyes on the Lord. Lean on
Him. Accept help. Learn what He wants you to know.

What is your trial today? And what is your need in that trial?
Do you need someone to pray for you? Then share your difficulty
with a Christian. Do you need wisdom in your situation? Reach
out and ask others for help and direction. Do you need a ride
to church...or to the hospital for your next treatment...or to the
airport because you don't have a car or yours won't start? Share
your need. Don't be too proud to divulge that you require help.
Let God use others to assist you as you make your way through
your trials. This shows your maturity and lets God work through
the other person. You both get blessed!

7. *Deception*. Solomon, the wisest man who ever lived before Christ came, observed, "The backslider in heart will be filled with his own ways" (Proverbs 14:14). He taught that those who wander away from the Lord will reap the consequences of that choice. As a woman who desires to find and stay on God's path through the thick and thin of life, you need to especially be on the alert for self-deception.

Do you know how we often step off God's path and fail to follow Him? By failing to obey God's precepts. When we've given way to one sin—any sin, however small or large—we have two action choices. We confess our wrongdoing, wrong choice, or wrong behavior and get back on God's path, or we deceive ourselves about the offense, refuse to consider change, and put off any positive action. We excuse ourselves by saying, "It's not *that* bad. Everyone slips up once in a while. After all, as the Bible says, 'All have sinned'! And besides, it didn't hurt anybody. What's the big deal anyway?" Our rationalization for sin can go on and on. Yet God's Word says:

> *If we say that we have no sin, we deceive ourselves, and the truth is not in us.*
>
> *If we confess our sins, He is faithful and just to forgive us our sins and to cleanse us from all unrighteousness.*
>
> *If we say that we have not sinned, we make Him a liar, and His word is not in us* (1 John 1:8-10).

Think for a minute about King David and his sexual sin with Bathsheba, another man's wife. At first glance it might be easy to excuse his behavior: "Well, David must have had a weak area— women!" But when you back up in the account to see what led up to this sin, you discover that David may have had a problem *before* he saw Bathsheba...another kind of problem. The Bible reports: "At the time when kings go out to battle, that David sent Joab....But David remained at Jerusalem" (2 Samuel 11:1). I wonder, Was he being lazy? Tired? Depressed? Did he simply not feel like leading his people, going to war, and fulfilling his kingly responsibilities?

That was Problem #1.

And Problem #2 swiftly arrived on his first problem's heels. While King David remained behind, with next to nothing to do but stroll on his rooftop, he saw Bathsheba bathing. In David we witness how one sin, left unchecked and unacknowledged, can lead to the next sin, which can lead to the next and the next. David stayed behind, saw a married woman, asked about her, sent for her, slept with her, arranged for her husband's murder and then hid the crime. David looked. David lusted. David planned and executed adultery and a murder.

> God is willing and able to keep you on His path, right alongside Him, as you enter, endure, and exit your trials.

After these monstrous acts, he deceived himself for almost a year, covering up and covering over his many sins. He committed sin upon sin upon sin, adding layer upon layer upon layer to his original sin. His first deception led to plotting, which led to murder, which led to lying.

It's tempting to deceive ourselves into accepting unbiblical conduct by saying, "It's okay" or "It's not so bad" instead of being mature, putting on the brakes, and doing the right thing. Obedience is a sign of a follower of Christ. When we fail to follow His instructions and principles, God provides a way for us to return to His path. What are we to do? We are to pray, to admit our failure to follow God, and to agree with God about our sinfulness. Then His wonderful forgiveness is ours!

This is how you get right back on God's path. And prayer, sweet prayer...also *keeps* you there! When you take your problems and trials to your heavenly Father, He is faithful to help you resist and triumph over greed, jealousy, strife, self-confidence, temptation, laziness, lies...and the whole list of sins we are so prone to commit. God is willing and able to keep you on His path, right alongside Him, as you enter, endure, and exit your trials. And what awaits you on the other side?

❧ new depth of character

❧ a better understanding of God

❧ greater resistance to sin (thanks be to His grace!)

❧ a more intimate identity with Christ

❧ a more positive approach to and anticipation of the future

This, my friend, is spiritual maturity, a maturity that makes you more productive and useful to the Lord and to others. The ultimate test of life is usefulness, so be sure to deal with any and all roadblocks that hinder your progress.

Letting God Work in You

We've spent several chapters focusing on reasons we don't allow God to work in us, on why we don't yield to His testing. Now let's make a 180-degree turn. Let's let go of our fears and doubts about our trials and go with God's plan.

God wants us to surrender to our trials, to submit to them with no resistance whatsoever. He wants us to allow Him to work in us. All we have to do is bend...just bend. We're not going to break. Really! God's goal is not to break us but to make us into more mature Christians—useful and stable. So accept His trials. He's not asking you to give up. Just give in to the tests He brings and take the steps He's asking of you. The grace He promises to give will come as you move forward in obedience.

When it comes to letting and yielding and submitting to God, I envision an altar. Each day I try to spiritually and mentally climb up on the altar and lie down. There I am, lying face up—face-to-face with God—opening up my heart and clenched fists to Him. It is an official time of yielding, of giving everything to Him. I pray, "Here I am, Lord. Take me—*all* of me. This is Your day and Your life. I am Your servant. Help Yourself to every aspect of my life. I am presenting myself to you as a living sacrifice."

For me this prayer, this formal release I offer to God helps me yield to His will—and trials!—for my day and my life. I got this idea from a seminar I attended some years ago called "Successful, Fulfilled Womanhood." The instructor, Verna Birkey, talked about "prayers of commitment" and prayers for releasing our rights. For instance, one suggested prayer was for single women: "Lord, help Yourself to my life. Whatever You choose, God." Do you sense the letting go expressed in "help Yourself," which is spoken in earnest to God? And married women, in addition to praying, "Help yourself to my life," also can pray, "and help Yourself to my husband's life too."

In the same way we need to yield to the testing God brings to help us mature. We need to defer to Him. Deferring is "yielding or submitting in recognition of another's authority." (That would certainly be God!) The definition goes on: "yielding or submitting in recognition of another's authority or superior knowledge." (Again, that would certainly be God!)

—*Taking a Step Forward*—

If you want to grow spiritually, roadblocks must be removed! So take this first step: *Yield* to God. Heave a sigh of relief and a sigh of release. Embrace the testing God brings into your life.

And here's a second step: *Know* that the testing of your faith works patience (James 1:3). Stay in your trials and "let patience have its perfect work" (1:4). The only positive way out of a trial is through it. So be done with manipulation and doing things your way by getting into and out of things such as commitments and responsibilities.

The third step? *Stay* in the trial because you desire what's on the other side. One reason for staying is to see that a *thorough* work is accomplished...and that requires all-the-way-to-the-end perseverance.

None know what they can bear
until they are tried.

Susanna Wesley

12

Experiencing God's Power and Perfection

❧

*So let [endurance] grow, for when your endurance is
fully developed, you will be strong in character
and ready for anything.*

James 1:4 NLT

Did your high school have a wrestling team? Did you or do you know a wrestler? An amazing fact about wrestlers is they can train, lift weights, and do body-building exercises, but until they actually wrestle opponents, they will never develop the skills wrestlers need.

The same is true of you and me in the spiritual realm. We can read God's Word, go to Bible studies, memorize scriptures, attend church and Sunday school, but until we actually face trials, we will not have the opportunity to use the faith and trust in God we're developing through these spiritual activities. Without experience we won't know how to best use the knowledge we're accumulating. We won't have the opportunity to develop staying power and spiritual maturity.

Letting God Work in Me

God works through trials in our lives to "perfect" and mature us. One "opponent" that really stands out as a benchmark in my life helped me change my lifestyle. I had a general tendency to be meticulous and careful as a person and as a time manager. You might say I was a "type A" personality. I've always had my schedule and my little routines so down to the minute that you could set a clock by them. But God had a few new things He wanted to teach me. So He began working on my attitude and my time management. How did He do this? By a trial, a test: He sent my family to the mission field. To Singapore, to be exact!

Little did I know when we landed in Singapore that my life was on the brink of major change. Jim and I and our two preteen daughters lived without a car. Can you imagine the trauma that was for someone who had lived in Los Angeles County where the locals almost live in their cars? What having no car meant was hours spent every day standing on corners waiting for buses that were always late or never came at all. I also stood at corners waving for taxis that wouldn't pull over because they were usually full. I stood in the rain with no transportation and no phone. (This was before cell phones became so affordable.) My perfect little routine I had so carefully developed over the decades was completely knocked out.

> *I had to learn to hand more and more of the undone things in my schedule to Him and relinquish more and more things in my precious routine.*

How did I respond to this new challenge and the trials associated with my situation? Friend, God wanted to move me toward perfection, which required transplanting me to Singapore. There in my "trial" He taught me variety—a variety of tailor-made trials, a variety of ways of living, and a variety of ways of managing. I learned that millions of women live in a way I'd never experienced. I also realized that a great deal of my teaching materials and focus couldn't be used effectively by the multitude of women who lived such different lifestyles than I was used to.

So there in that foreign country I learned to be flexible. I grew in patience as I became more and more accustomed to standing and waiting. A greater trust in God developed as I began to surrender—to yield—to His wisdom and purpose in my new living style. I grew to rest in the Lord, to hand more and more of the undone things in my schedule to Him, to relinquish more and more things in my precious routine, to let Him have His perfect work in me.

When my family returned to America, I came back a better person, a stronger Christian, a more sensitive servant of the Lord, and a more effective encourager of women in my teaching ministry. I also modified my teaching materials so I could reach a wider circle of women with God's messages of love, hope, strength, grace, and mercy.

This is just a simple example in my life of how God used trials to melt me, mold me, and grow me in Him. Praise the Lord!

God's Power Revealed

It's truly amazing to notice how God breaks us out of what we are comfortable with and moves us beyond our current state. He uses trials and tests to help us face and overcome challenges so we can do even greater feats for Him. Yes, these lessons don't come easily or cheaply. They develop and require fortitude, trust in God, and endurance until growth takes place. Then we have a better understanding of God's power and how to use it and count on it in future trials.

Take a minute to be inspired by the faith, endurance, and devotion to God exhibited by these people...who really were just like you and me. They found themselves in hard situations and had a choice in how to respond. And God honored their faith!

In the lions' den. Daniel was an Israelite who was taken captive to Babylon. He was very gifted and soon gained the king's trust and favor. In time, the court officials burned with envy and plotted to destroy the young Israelite. The end result was that Daniel was sealed into a den of lions to be killed and eaten.

But Daniel trusted God. He knew God would not abandon him. In the lions' den Daniel witnessed the power of God and the presence of one of God's angels! As Daniel later explained to the king, "My God sent His angel and shut the lions' mouths, so that they have not hurt me, because I was found innocent before Him" (Daniel 6:22).

And so the miracle occurred. Daniel lived untouched and unharmed, God was glorified, and worship took place. The king himself wrote to the people, "The God of Daniel...is the living God, and steadfast forever...and He works signs and wonders: [and] has delivered Daniel from the power of the lions" (verses 26-27). As Daniel endured and stayed through his ordeal in the lions' den, unbelievers witnessed God's power, Daniel's faith in God was further strengthened, and he went on to receive some of the greatest revelations of future events ever given by God to any person.

In the fire. Shadrach, Meshach, and Abed-Nego, three of Daniel's friends were tried by fire. They were thrown into a furnace for refusing to bow and worship a gold image, as the king had commanded (Daniel 3:1-19). These three men willingly accepted their trial and then experienced the power of God *and* the presence of God through a fourth "man" who appeared in the fire with them. The king described this "man": "like the Son of God" (verses 24-26). This figure is believed by most scholars to have been the pre-incarnate Christ.

And the results of Shadrach, Meshach, and Abed-Nego's time in the fire? God was glorified and witnessed! Shadrach, Meshach, and Abed-Nego came out of the furnace untouched. Their faith was strengthened by God's powerful ability to deliver them (verse 17). And the miracle was witnessed and proclaimed by the king to the people: "Blessed be the God of Shadrach, Meshach and Abednego, who sent His Angel and delivered His servants who trusted in Him. There is no other God who can deliver like this" (verses 28-29). Afterwards these three Israelites were given positions of importance and continued to be a living testimony to a living God.

On the altar. After 25 years of waiting, Abraham finally had a son by Sarah. But Abraham's testing was definitely not over. After some years, God asked His servant, Abraham, to offer his son Isaac on the altar as a burnt offering to Him. What a test! But Abraham stepped into the waters of this test, took his son to the prescribed spot, bound him, and placed him on an altar.

As Abraham followed through and lifted the knife to slay his son, a miracle occurred…but not until the last possible second! God spoke out of heaven and commanded Abraham not to kill his son. Next He provided a sacrifice—a ram tangled in a nearby bush (Genesis 2:2-14).

Yes, the wondrous miracle occurred—in Isaac's life and Abraham's. God is faithful to His people—including us! He uses His power to take us through—or get us out of!—our trials. Abraham's faith never budged. He passed the test!

Abraham stands as a role model for us to persevere and follow God's leading. He was a model of genuine faith. He is called "the father of all those who believe" (Romans 4:11).

On the cross. And then we have the supreme example of Christ staying on the cross. A sinless man and the Son of God, Jesus fully bore the penalty of our sins on the cross. The sin of the world and the lies and treachery of people put Him there. But He chose to stay. He endured. Many, many miracles transpired as a result of His obedience to God: the miracle of darkness at noon; the miracle of the curtain in the temple being torn from top to bottom; the miracle of the dead rising; the miracle of Jesus' resurrection; and especially the miracle of redemption and salvation for us.[2] He stayed on the cross even when taunted by "He saved others; Himself He cannot save. If He is the King of Israel, let Him now come down from the cross" (Matthew 27:42). We know that as God, Jesus Christ most definitely could have come down, but He persevered, thus fulfilling God's desire for our redemption. He did the Father's will, fully trusting in Him, committing Himself to the God who judges righteously (1 Peter 2:23).

> *At the end of your trial or testing, you will know God more intimately, your faith will be strengthened, and your Christian character will be sterling.*

In all of these instances the people being tested stayed, and miracles occurred. Also in these situations, God was glorified. And in every incident faith was matured because God did the miracles and everyone knew He did them. It was clearly God to the rescue! God with the solutions! It was 100 percent Him and not the skills, knowledge, abilities, smooth talking, and clever manipulations of humans that ended these tests. Those involved only had to do three things: step into their test, stay in their test, and wait on and trust in God.

That's your test too. When a trial arrives (and you know it will!), stay in it. At the end of your trial or testing, you will know God more intimately, your faith will be strengthened, and your Christian character will be sterling. Greater maturity and more ministry await you, along with stronger endurance. The blessings are countless!

How Long Can You Stay?

I have a big question for you: How long can you stay in a trial? Walking through the Old Testament, we see that...

Noah, by faith, preached for 120 years while he was building the ark. How long would you stay faithful and continue to articulate God's truth to people who disdained you and wrote you off as a nut?

Abraham, who lived 170 years, was sent out by God to search for a city. Abraham obeyed, not knowing where he was going...and died in faith, never having received the promise, never even seeing the city he searched for. How long would you have searched?

Leah, who was plain-looking, and her beautiful sister, Rachel, were married to the same man, Jacob. But the Bible says Jacob loved Rachel. How long would you stay in a loveless marriage? Dear Leah stayed...and in the end was blessed by being the mother of six sons who eventually represented six of the 12 tribes of Israel. She grew in maturity and reaped her rewards for staying.

Ruth too was a woman who stayed—not in a place, but with a person—with her bitter mother-in-law. Naomi, whose name means "pleasant," told the people, "Do not call me Naomi; call me Mara," which means "bitter" (Ruth 1:20). Ruth left her family, her home, and everything else to follow Naomi to her homeland, staying by her anguished mother-in-law's side. And the outcome? She married a godly man and bore a son who was in the line of the Messiah.

Abigail stayed in an unpleasant marriage. She was married to a foolish, alcoholic man and spent her married life righting his wrongs and their disastrous consequences. The result of her faithfulness, stability, wisdom, and maturity gained from remaining in her situation? She married King David after her husband's death.

And more recently…

Susanna Wesley was in a challenging and difficult marriage. In a biographical sketch about her life entitled "A House Divided," We discover Susanna persevered and did her best. Her gifts had to shine through the clouded window of her marriage. She used her strong leadership talents in training well-educated and disciplined children, including John and Charles Wesley. Susanna could say with assurance, "None knows what they can bear until they are tried." Rather than succumb to despair, this woman of faith put her energies into raising a house full of well-behaved, spiritually sensitive children. She honored her husband's strengths and she forgave him his faults, year after difficult year. In addition to her rigorous home duties, this talented lady took on other projects that brought fulfillment to her life. She wrote three religious books for children, and her home became a center of encouragement and spiritual ministry in the community. Though her world was small and its walls may have seemed high, she flourished in its confines.[2]

Susanna Wesley stayed…and she bore much fruit.

Moving Toward Perfection

Staying, staying, staying. There is no other way to go through God's tests, witness His power, experience His perfection, and partake of His blessings of greater growth and contribution. After much study on the three terms or results of God's testing—"perfect, entire, lacking nothing"—I realized they are basically the same. There are some variations, but the point is that maturity and usefulness are the overarching outcomes of trials endured and seen through to the end. Through trials and testing we become...

..."perfect." An Old Testament sacrifice had to be a perfect animal—one that was fit to be sacrificed to God: no blemishes, broken bones, maiming, blindness, disease, or anything lacking in its parts (Leviticus 22).

..."entire" or whole or complete or fully developed. To be so requires perfection in all the parts or portions with no defects, no missing parts.

..."lacking in nothing." To be so means wanting to be without any defect and deficient in nothing.

I encourage you to persevere. When times get tough, talk to God. Share your thoughts and feelings with Him. He will understand. He won't get upset. And He will give you the strength you need to continue.

—Taking a Step Forward—

Are you wondering (as I constantly do), "How can I stay in my trials?" And then, "How can I stay there longer?" In other words, "What does it take to stay?" By now you know the answers!

Step 1: Approach each trial with a joyful attitude. "Count it all joy." If you can face and conquer this hurdle, you will be walking through your trial by the Holy Spirit!

Step 2: Remember God's power. When your trial gets harder and the steps grow steeper, you struggle. Remind yourself, "Is anything too hard for the LORD?" (Genesis 18:14) and remember the answer: "Ah, Lord GOD! Behold, You have made the heavens and the earth by Your great power and outstretched arm. There is nothing too hard for You" (Jeremiah 32:17).

Step 3: Pray. Prayer keeps you looking to God, who has promised that He will finish what He's started. Wonderful! We can be "confident of this very thing, that He who has begun a good work in you [such as asking you to go through a trial] will complete it" (Philippians 1:6). Prayer also keeps you looking to Jesus, the author and finisher of your faith (Hebrews 12:2). He endured the cross, and you can't be looking at God and looking at Jesus and not experience the victory of endurance in your trial.

Step 4: Sit quietly. Yield. Let God work in you. You can keep slinging the dishes, slamming the drawers and doors, and stomping through life...or you can stop, sit down, and ask God, "All right, Lord. What do You want? What is the lesson here? What would You have me do, think, say, be?" Sit quietly in God's presence and allow Him to answer and help you stay in your trial clear through to the end.

Step 5: Focus on God's promises. To begin this step, take 1 Corinthians 10:13 to heart. Here God promises that if your trial or situation becomes more than you can bear, He will provide a way of escape so you can bear it. He won't give you more than you can handle!

Dear reader, "Let patience have its perfect work, that you may be perfect and complete, lacking nothing" (James 1:4). And remember, God's ways are not our ways, and His thoughts are not our thoughts. An anonymous poem beautifully sums up these thoughts and our pilgrimage from infancy to maturity:

> I asked God for strength that I might achieve,
> I was made weak that I might learn to humbly obey.

I asked for help that I might do greater things,
I was given infirmity that I might do better things.

I asked for riches that I might be happy,
I was given poverty that I might be wise.

I asked for power that I might have the praise of men,
I was given weakness so that I might feel the need of God.

I asked for all things that I might enjoy life,
I was given life that I might enjoy all things.

I got nothing that I asked for but everything I had hoped
for.
I am among all men, most richly blessed.

Section 4

Becoming a Mighty Woman

*God's ways of answering His people's prayers
is not by removing the pressure,
but by increasing their strength to bear it.*[1]

13

Finding Strength in God's Grace

ﷺ

And [the Lord] said to me, "My grace is sufficient for you,
for My strength is made perfect in weakness."
Therefore most gladly I will rather boast in my infirmities,
that the power of Christ may rest upon me.

2 Corinthians 12:9

I'm sure you've heard of Wonder Woman and Superwoman. What little—or big!—girl hasn't? They are indeed a dynamic duo and quite the examples to live up to! Many of us grew up with these two superheroes looming in front of us. And we try to emulate their strength and valor on a lesser scale in our not-so-super daily lives. Like them, we attempt to accomplish the impossible...only our failure rate is off the scale.

Personally I would much rather be "a mighty woman." By that I mean I would rather be a woman who, no matter how weak or limited, is filled with the power of God, a woman who is strengthened with His glorious might, a woman who labors and strives according to God's power, which works mightily in her. That's what I want—and need—for myself, especially when the trials come.

Responding to Trials and Tribulations

So far we have learned that trials are a reality of everyday life. But, praise God, we can be joyful in them. In addition, we know that two grand qualities—stability and endurance—result from tests of faith. And we've grasped that tests lead to spiritual and personal maturity and usefulness that cannot be gained any other way. So why don't we always treasure trials? Welcome them? Embrace them? To put it bluntly, trials are often painful and usually frustrating.

> *Rather than questioning and asking for an explanation from God, we can look to Him for strength and endure to the end.*

Let's look at three avoidance responses to trials: escape, explain, and exit.

Escape—We're often willing to do almost anything to keep from going through a trial. No one *wants* to suffer. And no one wants to *endure* difficult situations. So we try to sidestep or get out of trials. Do you remember Jonah? This is how he reacted when asked by God to take a message of redemption to the people in Ninevah—he tried to escape by heading in the opposite direction...away from Ninevah (Jonah 1:1-3).

But since we now recognize that staying in our trials is what perfects and matures us, hopefully our attitude is changing.

Explain—When the road gets rough and the going gets tough, it's natural to start asking God, "Why, why, oh why, did this have to happen to me?" Job was guilty of this reaction as he tried to explain to his friends—and to God!—why he didn't deserve to be in his condition of pain and suffering (Job 29–31).

Rather than questioning and asking for an explanation from God, we can accept what is happening to us because we know it is for a good cause, look to God for strength, and endure to the end.

Exit—When in pain, the first thing we want to do is get out of it...and the sooner the better! This response can lead us to lie, manipulate, drop out, avoid certain people...anything to exit the painful experience. Abraham was guilty of this response as he left the land God had promised him to travel to Egypt during a famine. And what did he do in Egypt? He lied about who his wife was and tried to manipulate his situation to avoid trials (Genesis 12:10-13).

Yet Christ our Savior willingly *endured* the pain of the cross and separation from God. We can endure our trials too. By God's grace and with His help, we can continue on His path through our trials and grow in the areas He knows are lacking.

So what responses should we have when we encounter a trial?

❧ *Be joyful*—This is a choice, not an emotion. We can think, *Oh boy! Another chance to grow more like Jesus. Another opportunity to bring honor to Him. Another way to increase my faith and trust in God.*

❧ *Believe*—This is also a decision we make. We decide to think, *Just think, God promises I'll be more faithful and stable on the other side of this trial.*

❧ *Bend*—There's one more decisive action we can

take. We can think, *Have thine own way, Lord!*[2] *Help Yourself to my life. Teach me. Grow me. Use me.*

Finding Strength in Weakness

In addition to the teachings of James 1:2-4, there is another scripture I draw upon every time I'm faced with a trial. No matter what is happening to me, what I am up against, what is breaking my heart, or what I am suffering, I turn to the strength offered and assured in 2 Corinthians 12:9. These words of promise are spoken by Christ Himself: "My grace is sufficient for you, for My strength is made perfect in weakness."

Wow! Who doesn't need this kind of assurance in a trial? For more than 2,000 years this pledge from God has helped Christians endure everything life and the world can throw at them. The apostle Paul is a great example.

Paul was God's servant, but the believers in Corinth were questioning his sincerity and authenticity as an apostle. Therefore Paul wrote to defend and prove himself to his opponents. In doing so, he basically said, "Well, there is one really big thing I could brag about if I needed to." Then Paul described a vision he was allowed to see and hear when he was miraculously "caught up to heaven" (2 Corinthians 12:2). It was indeed glorious, but Paul explains that because he could have been exalted by others and filled with personal pride due to this supernatural experience, "a thorn in the flesh was given to me, a messenger of Satan to buffet me, lest I be exalted above measure" (verse 7).

We don't know exactly what Paul's thorn in the flesh was, but it was probably painful or frustrating. And how did Paul handle this? He did what we would have done—he prayed. He asked God three times to take away the exasperating problem. But God's way of answering Paul's prayers was not by removing the pressure. Instead, God increased Paul's strength to bear it!

And how did Paul's story of pain and suffering end? He spells out how the Lord spoke words of encouragement to him so he could stay in his hardship and keep on serving Christ and His followers. Paul reports...

> And [the Lord] said to me, "My grace is sufficient for you, for My strength is made perfect in weakness." Therefore most gladly [Paul concludes] I will rather boast in my infirmities, that the power of Christ may rest upon me. Therefore I take pleasure in infirmities, in reproaches, in needs, in persecutions, in distresses, for Christ's sake. For when I am weak, then I am strong (2 Corinthians 12:9-10).

Paul had a problem—a thorn in his flesh. It was a trial. And whatever it was, it hurt or bothered him so much that he referred to it as a literal "stake."[3] He felt like he was impaled on a sharpened pole. Furthermore, the source of that thorn in his flesh was Satan. But Paul knew to look on both sides of the coin: He saw one side—Satan's image—but he also turned the coin of pain and suffering over to see the impression of God, the imprint of the One who permitted the trial...and promised to see him through it.

And the purpose of the trial? Paul repeats it twice: It was sent as a guard against pride, which would have been a detriment to his personal life, his ministry, and his relationship with God.

Staying on God's Path

From the 2 Corinthians 12:7-10 passage, you can immediately learn a few things about enduring trials and continuing on God's path through every trial.

First, God's grace is *sufficient,* meaning it is enough. His grace is all you need in any and all trials. And it is not only *all* you need, it is also *what* you need. It is a treasure of various kinds and various colors from which you may obtain the materials that will match

> *We don't need to worry or wonder or try to peek around corners to see if God's grace is going to be there when we face a difficulty. Why? Because it's already there!*

any circumstance and repair any disaster into which you've fallen. And it will be there, *when* you need it. God never delays, but He also is never hurried. His grace will take you to—and through— the stretching point, the breaking point, the giving-up and giving-in point, and the falling-apart point. He sometimes waits for the moment of extreme pressure…and then gloriously, as promised, steps in with *what* you need *when* you need it.

Second, *God's power dwells in you*. His grace is the source of your might. Through the power of God's grace you become a mighty woman, one who can face, handle, and endure whatever happens.

And here's another truth: God gives as much of His marvelous grace as you require. He gives it abundantly.

The spiritually mature woman can do and make it through anything and everything, whether it is bearing burdens, doing more than she's accustomed to, or doing something special God is asking her to do. An anonymous poet wrote:

> My Lord never said that He would give
> Another's grace without another's thorn.
> What matter, since for every day of mine
> Sufficient grace comes for me with the morn.

> And though the future brings some heavier cross,
> I need not crowd the present with my fears:
> I know the grace that is enough today
> Will be sufficient still through all the years.[4]

When it comes to God's sufficiency and God's grace, we don't need to worry or wonder or try to peek around the corners to see if His grace is going to be there when we face a difficulty. Why? Because it's already there! God's grace will be all you need, will be what you need, will be as much as you need, will be complete.

Recounting God's Grace

God's grace was sufficient for Daniel in the lions' den and for his three friends in the furnace (Daniel 6:16-22; 3:19-27). For Hannah too as she handed over her only child, her little Samuel, to Eli (1 Samuel 1:10-28). Also for Sarah and Elizabeth as they remained barren into their senior years (Genesis 18:13; Luke 1:36). As well as for Esther and Eunice, who lived with unbelieving husbands (Esther 1:19–2:17; 2 Timothy 1:5). For Leah as she was locked in a loveless marriage (Genesis 29:30). For Priscilla as she and her husband were driven from their home (Acts 18:2). For Mary, the mother of Jesus, as she watched her son—our Messiah and Savior—die (John 19:23,25).

Each of these people found the strength and might in God's grace that was needed for their trials…

…and the same will be true for you.

–Taking a Step Forward –

What difficulty are you in or up against today that you wonder how you will ever get through it?

Right this minute my current trials include encouraging and supporting a brother who is going through cancer treatments, meeting a tough book deadline, fulfilling an extra-full speaking season, and making peace with the physical distance between my

11 children and grandchildren (they live on the East Coast while Jim and I reside on the West Coast). Each of these trials requires leaning on God and looking to Him for His strength and grace.

From other friends and acquaintances came this sampling of trials:

❧ a single woman with car problems

❧ a career woman who daily goes to a job she dislikes and where she is ill-treated

❧ a family reeling under the surprise of a large tax bill

❧ an elderly woman facing painful—and painfully long—dental surgery

❧ a wife whose husband broke his leg in a friendly game of volleyball. His injury created significant loss of income and my friend will miss time from work for hospital visits and to eventually provide basic nursing care at home

❧ a young wife yearning for a child but going through her third miscarriage

❧ a wife (with four little ones!) whose husband's job takes him away from home months at a time

❧ a woman whose husband unexpectedly filed for divorce

❧ a wife who asked for prayer because her husband walked out after 40 years of marriage and moved to a foreign country

Your trial—correction: make that *trials!*—may differ from these, but as you now know trials, come in all shapes and sizes. But

God never does. He is unchanging. And His grace is always available and granted to His children as they struggle under their burdens.

God's promise extends to you. His grace is sufficient for *you,* in your own personal and unique set of circumstances and difficulties...even as they change throughout the day. And, dear one, His grace will always be available and sufficient.

To take a step forward, personalize this magnificent verse filled with truth and promise. Owning it for yourself: "And He said to *me,* 'My grace is sufficient, for My strength is made perfect in weakness'" (2 Corinthians 12:9). Yes, this powerful promise was spoken to the apostle Paul of Tarsus, but it extends individual encouragement to each of God's people, including you! So remember it. Use it. Repeat it. Count on it.

The power of God is also yours for the permanent trials, for the lasting physical affliction or disability, for unchangeable illness or weakness, for the unalterable life adjustments that come your way. God's power is sufficient for strengthening you for every trial...every minute...every day...for as long as it takes.

14

Counting on God's Power

~

And [the Lord] has said to me, "My grace is sufficient for you,
for power is perfected in weakness."
Most gladly, therefore, I will rather boast about my weaknesses,
so that the power of Christ may dwell in me.

2 Corinthians 12:9 NASB

One of my passions is being a mother to my two daughters, two sons-in-law, and now a grandmother to their seven little ones. Actually my feeling is better described as *fierce* passion! For the past three decades I have studied the Bible and read voraciously on being a mom. I've also researched and written much about this vital role of being a Christian mom to assist other moms out there who might need help like I did.[1]

There is one statement I found during my studies that has really stayed with me over the years: "Weakness always appeals to our sympathy. Ask the careful mother which child receives the greatest share of her thoughts and attention. It is not the one who is strong, and able to take care of himself, but the sickly and weak one, that is pressed closest to the mother's heart."[2]

Gaining Something Better

As I think about this insight right now, I can't help but think about God's love for us and His promise in 2 Corinthians 12:9: "My gracious favor is all you need. My power works best in your weakness" (NLT). God doesn't promise us a carefree life. But He does hold those who are hurting close to His heart. Ever merciful, His eyes and ears are always open to His needy loved ones (1 Peter 3:12). Ever giving, God blesses His weak children with the priceless gifts of His own strength and power.

Jesus spoke this assurance to His faithful—and suffering—servant Paul. The apostle Paul was one of God's mightiest spokesmen, yet he became weakened by some affliction or difficulty. After praying fervently for the removal of his "thorn in the flesh," Paul received God's answer. Rather than take away Paul's cause of pain, our all-wise, compassionate God elected to give him something far better than smooth sailing. He chose to provide Paul with all the strength he would ever need to *endure* his immediate agony…and make it through to the other side. And God promised Paul—and us!—all the strength he would ever need to endure and triumph over all the suffering, hardships, and trials we endure. God imparted *His* might to Paul to fortify him *while* he suffered.

It is clear that God closed the door on a pain-free and trouble-free life for Paul. Instead He granted him His all-sufficient grace for every minute and every need in his life. Instead of sending help through other means, the Lord showered His servant with His great and marvelous grace! Paul would have something *better* than a breezy existence: He would have all he ever needed from God to face all that he encountered so he would mature spiritually. In his weakness Paul had God's power to endure, move forward, and triumph. Instead of taking away Paul's problem, Christ blessed Paul with grace to get through it.

The result? Paul gained something significantly better than temporary relief in a trial. He gained the power of Christ. As theologian Charles Ryrie notes, "The power of Christ in Paul was more important than freedom from pain."[3]

Putting Weakness to Work

An interesting facet of God's power is that it is perfected in our weakness. Amazingly, when we are weak and suffering and in need, God's power is there. In fact, His strength finds its full scope in our weakness. Actually the word for "weakness" used in 2 Corinthians 12:9 is "strengthlessness." Have you ever felt strengthless—like you had no strength at all? Well, good news! Your strengthlessness is the very element that allows God's power to be exhibited more perfectly in your life. This brings us down to a choice. Who will be supreme? Will it be "He" or "me"? Will I rely on God and His power and grace...or will I continue to rely on my personal resources and abilities?

D.L. Moody, a remarkable and well-known preacher from the past, said, "In

> *God's way is not always to take His children out of trials, but instead to give them the strength to bear the trials.*

the divine partnership, we contribute weakness." God contributes all the strength while we so easily and constantly contribute weakness as we face our trials and His plan for our lives. It takes *our weakness* to become aware of our need for *His strength*. And it is *our weakness* that shows *His strength* in us! Therefore, when we are weak, we are really strong and mighty and powerful because God's strength is revealed—fulfilled and completed and shown most effective. Put another way, *God's power* comes to its full strength or finds its full scope in *our weakness*. All that we are able to handle and endure is because of Him. Enduring and succeeding is all by and of His grace, His sufficiency, His strength, His power, which stands in remarkable contrast to our absolute weakness.

How does this work personally? I realized that I am the weak one in the relationship I have with God. He is the powerful one, the mighty one. And while my trial endures, His grace endures as well. My strength is God's rival, it hides or covers His work…but my weakness is His servant, it allows His power to shine through.

God's way is not always to take His children out of trials but instead to give them the strength to bear the trials. This needs to be our preferred condition because it allows God to be revealed and us to grow spiritually strong.

Putting God's Strength to Work at Home

Like most women, I especially need to call upon God's grace in my daily duties. You know, those mundane tasks, routine things I have to do for a great part of my life. For instance, I remember when my daughters, who are only 13 months apart, were young. It seemed like there were four years when all I did was discipline them. I would get up and pray I wouldn't have to discipline them that day: "Today, dear Lord, please, just for today, let it be a nice day!" But by the time the day was over I felt like I hadn't been a mom at all. Instead, I had been a sheriff or referee, towering over my little girls all day, dishing out instructions and reproofs: Don't do that! Stop doing that! Go to your room! I'm going to discipline you!

I can still remember reminding myself, "I have got to do this now while they are young. This is what a mom does when her children are at this stage. If I don't do it now, we'll all pay later." That was also the season when I felt like the only word I knew, said, or heard all day, every day was "No!" My toddlers would say *no* to me, and I would say *no* to them. It even got down to "No, you're not going to say *no* to me!" It seemed like all I did was discipline day in and day out, from sunrise to sunset.

In truth, I didn't desire to train my children nor did I actually know how if I did choose to. I felt so inadequate, and in my times of weakness I so wanted to give up. But God impressed upon me the importance of my faithfulness through His Word. So I depended on and drew upon His grace. And He enabled me to follow through and stay faithful during those tough years.

And there are so many other duties and responsibilities women have. There's the housework that's never done. The challenge of caring for the people who are in our homes. Whether those people are family, guests, elderly relatives or friends, ill or dying folks, we get up every day and face them. They're right in front of us! And don't forget preparing meals, meals, and more meals. Setting more tables. Washing more dishes. Wiping down more counters. Dealing with more garbage. Sometimes when I think of the kitchen I screech, "Eek!" because there is always work to be done there. Something needs to be put away, something needs to be cleaned, something has to be done to get the next meal started.

And do I even need to say anything about the never-ending laundry? I recall author Elisabeth Elliot talking about visiting her daughter and her eight children. Mrs. Elliot asked her daughter, "What is the worst thing you face in having this many children?" Her answer? "The constant laundry. It's never all done, it's never all folded, it's never all ironed, and it's never all put away." Well put! (And by the way, this was Mrs. Elliot's clue as to the best way to help her daughter during her visit. She washed, folded, ironed, and put away clothes while she was there.)

Do you think dealing with the daily duties at home—taking care of the people and the place—requires God's grace? Yes! It's His assignment for us—and yes, it has its rewards, but it is tiring and sometimes discouraging and seemingly impossible. Praise God His grace comes to the rescue when we are dead tired, pressed for time, and disheartened by mundane chores.

The Scope of Life's Challenges

God's power and grace is sufficient for the many unexpected crises and challenges that come our way. My family has personally experienced a typhoon, a 6.8 killer earthquake, the terrorist attack on The World Trade Center on September 11, 2001, a hurricane, a house fire, many ice storms, and numerous extended power outages. How about you? Are you familiar with this scene? The phone rings and it's the doctor who has frightening test results for you. (And you thought you were just having a "routine" test done!) Or an aging parent calls with more bad health news. Or the hospital a parent was checked into calls to let you know of a medical emergency. Or the police contact you, telling you a loved one has been in a car wreck. Or your neighbor calls to say something's wrong at her house and will you please come over...or call the police...or call the ambulance. Praise God His strength and power are available during the crises and disasters!

> *God's strength enables you to stay, to remain, to endure, to work, to assist others, to see all things through to the end.*

The power of God is yours for the permanent trials, for the lasting physical affliction or disability, for unchangeable illness or weakness, for the unalterable life adjustments that come your way. God's power is sufficient for strengthening you for every trial...every minute...every day...for as long as it takes.

God's grace is also sufficient for the things that are fleeting, that come and go. Power is there when you need it, as much as you need it, and at the time you need it. Strength is available for finishing whatever needs to be finished. God takes your weaknesses and inabilities and fills and replaces them with His almighty power. His strength enables you to stay, to remain, to endure, to work, to assist others, to see all things through to the end.

The amazing power of the God who created the universe is also sufficient and available for new starts. Sometimes God has us leave the familiar and start over in a new home, in a new church, in a new city (or country), in a new neighborhood. Our children start all over again in a different school. Or we start over again in a new job...or a new marriage. Or we must start up again after a long illness or recovery. As we face an unknown future wrought with unfamiliar challenges, we face its newness with our familiar, never-changing God, along with all His power and might. No matter how fearful we are...or sad...or how deeply we dread... or how broken our hearts, God is there to empower us to see it through. He will give us His strength. God promises it and provides it. And He always will.

—Taking a Step Forward—

Do you now know what the secret to being a mighty woman boils down to? It is what I call a "He–me" realization. He is strong and sufficient...and I am not. So I have a choice to make. I can lean on and depend on and receive His all-sufficient, all-powerful grace...or I can lean on and depend on myself, a losing proposition for sure! And the same is true for you. Whatever the challenge or hurdle in your life, whatever temptation comes, whatever impossibility you are facing, whatever overwhelming physical or emotional stress plagues your life, remember—God's grace and power are sufficient. Such awesome, glorious, miraculous truths cannot be stated more simply, positively, and powerfully: God gives His grace and power to you!

So how can you incorporate this into your life? How can you tap into God's power for your daily issues and life's struggles?

Step 1: Memorize 2 Corinthians 12:9: "And He said to me, 'My grace is sufficient for you, for My strength is made perfect in weakness.' Therefore most gladly I will rather boast in my infirmities, that the power of Christ may rest upon me." God is powerful. His grace is powerful. And His Word is also more powerful than a two-edged sword (Hebrews 4:12). Once 2 Corinthians 12:9 is yours and in your heart—and arsenal!—whatever you face you can say, "Now remember, God says His grace is sufficient and His power will overshadow my weakness. Whatever this is, wherever it goes, whatever it brings, whatever is waiting for me when I get there, and however long it lasts, He gives me His grace. He will see me through."

Knowing and using this truth will help you approach difficulties with scriptural thoughts. Whatever is happening to you, or whatever you're up against, realize it is not overwhelming. It is not a total disaster. It is not the end. It is not impossible. It is not more than you can handle. Why? Because of God's grace and strength. This truth is a sword you can use as you fight depression, discouragement, anxiety, and fear. It is your balm as you live in pain, are in a painful situation, or cope with the pain birthed by something unjust or unfair.

Step 2: Realize this is a promise. When our children were young, Jim contributed to a Christian ministry and received as a thank-you gift a little plastic memory verse holder shaped like a loaf of bread. It came loaded with brightly colored cards—each bearing a verse of promise. We set it on the breakfast table, and each morning one of us would pick a promise from God from the little bread loaf and read it aloud. Now imagine yourself reaching into that loaf and discovering that every single card has the promise from 2 Corinthians 12:9 written on it. And every single day of your life you're reminded that indeed God's grace is sufficient for you! Okay. Now, don't just imagine it. Accept it. This is truth. It's real. Live it!

Step 3: Realize God's grace is a fact. He says His grace is sufficient. Therefore it is, and you can count on it. This promise is not about you—it's about Him. We know we're weak. But we can bank on the promise of His strength to see us through.

Step 4: Realize the truth that God's amazing grace is present when it seems nothing else is left. When there is no other hope, this truth is your hope. His grace is with you and is more than sufficient. There is no greater power available to you in this world!

You can count on it!

In the divine partnership,
we contribute weakness.[1]

D.L. MOODY

15

Drawing on God's Might

ॐ

But he said to me, "My grace is sufficient for you,
for my power is made perfect in weakness."
Therefore I will boast all the more gladly about my
weaknesses, so that Christ's power may rest on me.
That is why, for Christ's sake, I delight in weaknesses,
in insults, in hardships, in persecutions,
in difficulties.
For when I am weak, then I am strong.
2 Corinthians 12:9-10 NIV

ॐ One of the benefits of my years in the church choir was
getting to see those who attended both services each Sunday
morning. One person I noticed a lot was Mary, the wife of one of
my pastors. I never think about the scriptural concept of the power
of Christ "resting" on a person and it being so obvious that others
notice it without thinking of Mary. From the time I learned about
her husband's terminal cancer diagnosis, I watched this suffering
couple as they sat in the front row Sunday after Sunday.

I cannot begin to fully describe the impact their radiant lives had on me. I had more opportunities to be close to Mary than to her husband, so I witnessed firsthand God's strength in her. I saw how she bore all her dear one's tests and treatments, his hospitalizations, and his ever-present and ever-increasing pain. She faithfully and valiantly came alongside him, and I know that continued when they moved away to be closer to one of their sons and his family during Mary's husband's final days.

While they were at the church I would look at Mary and wonder, *How can she do this? How can she handle this? How can she bear this? How can she go through this?* And yet there she was every week, cheerful in her countenance, continuing in her ministries, living in faithfulness in every way, continuing to minister to others. She was such a visual testimony of Christ's glory and strength as she held up under the infirmities God sent. Everyone saw the evidence of the power of Christ "resting" or abiding on her (2 Corinthians 12:9). How did she do it? One of the things Mary did—and you and I need to do as well—was to acknowledge her trials.

Acknowledging Your Trials

Several chapters back we discussed some ways Christians avoid their problems. Well, that was not the case with Mary. She was not denying her problem or looking for a way out of or around her situation. No, she was looking for a way *through* it. She openly acknowledged the trials she and her husband were going through and was quick to ask for prayer. She also let others come alongside to help in different ways.

So let's take a cue from Mary. I ask you now, as we head into this new chapter about being a mighty woman—a woman of strength and power—to name the irritating, impossible, or unbearable thing you are dealing with, handling, or facing right now. You know, the one that's causing you the most thought. The one that stirs up the most pain, or distress, or worry, or sorrow. The one that bothers you the most. You might say it's the "hole in your bucket" that needs to be filled with God's joy, peace, and might. Your issue is always there. And it feels like all your energy is constantly leaking and draining out through the hole. Every time you think about your trial, or meet up with it again, there goes your joy, there goes your peace, there goes your contentment.

Recently I went through this same exercise myself, and I identified two issues. One of them is a "thing." It's the physical deterioration of a loved one. And short of a miracle from God it's not going to change for the better or go away. Every day when I wake up this life situation is the first thing I deal with spiritually, mentally, emotionally, and prayerfully. When I come face-to-face with this trial, I get strength for managing it one more day from 2 Corinthians 12:9: "And [Jesus] said to me, 'My grace is sufficient for you, for My strength is made perfect in weakness.'"

> *The power of the truths of God's grace and might causes our ordeals to fade into the shadows as the light is shifted from the problems and onto God's all-sufficient grace and strength.*

Amazingly, nothing more needs to be said or recalled to calm me. "My grace is sufficient for you." These are only six words out of the entire Bible, but they are six powerful words that change *me* in my situation in a second. The situation doesn't change, but the power of this truth about God's grace and might causes my ordeal to fade into the shadows as the light is shifted from the problem and onto God's all-sufficient grace and strength. Remembering the truth changes me *in* the situation.

My second daily challenge is a relationship. It's a person I meet face-to-face several times a week. And when I do, I think about the feelings that go with revisiting hard issues and difficult encounters in the past. And in this challenge I gain my might from the promise that God's grace is—and will be—all I need. Again I become calm. Nothing more needs to be said or done. Again, those six words change me and the relationship.

Think about it. What does it take in an intense relationship to smile, to be gracious, to be kind, to be pleasant, to be giving? It takes God's grace. And His grace is always there and always sufficient for us as we face difficulties...and difficult people!

A wonderful truth: Whether your problem is a particular situation or person, you will get the strength, might, power, wisdom, and grace from God to meet it head-on, endure, and triumph. God has promised it. You *will* make it! You *will* be able to handle it. You *will* be able to take it as it comes. You *will* get through it. You *will* have victory. Why? Because *God,* not you, supplies the all-sufficient grace that is needed.

So I ask you now: Can you ever encounter a trial or situation where God's grace will not be available or sufficient? The answer is never, never, never! His grace is a never-failing sufficiency. His grace was the source of my special friend Mary's might, and it will be the source of your strength as well.

Responding to God's Grace

After acknowledging our trial and God's all-sufficient grace, the next move to make is to respond to God's grace and might. What can we do, other than be in awe and give worship, thanksgiving, and praise? The apostle Paul tells us what his response was. He boldly and jubilantly declared, "Therefore most gladly I will rather boast in my infirmities, that the power of Christ may rest upon me" (2 Corinthians 12:9). As Paul dwelt on the paradox of his weakness and God's strength, he wholeheartedly accepted and embraced God's answer of "no" to his prayer that his "thorn in the flesh" be taken away from him. He totally and without reservation believed God's will was best for him—and that God's grace was indeed sufficient to help him bear his burden.

Paul not only submitted to God and to his malady, he *gladly* submitted, even to the point of boasting and bragging about his weakness. Paul gloried in his weakness! Why? Because in and through his weakness, Christ would powerfully work through him. Christ's power on full display through him, a weak vessel, would be like a spectacular light show! Paul was wise, knowledgeable, educated by the best of the best, a powerful lawyer and teacher, and blessed by his spectacular heritage and Jewish pedigree. But his weakness produced an even more powerful element in his life and testimony—the power of Christ at work.

> *What are the right responses to trials? Glory in them! Glory in Christ's covering! Glory in Christ's strength!*

And not only was God's spectacular, supernatural power at work and on display through Paul's infirmity, but it also "enshrined" him. It "rested" on him. It "tabernacled upon" him. It acted as "a shelter over" him. It overshadowed Paul's weakness and infirmity, causing his work and works to be 100 percent effective despite his problem and strengthlessness.

What are the right responses Paul gives us to ongoing trials?

Glory in them! Let your infirmities become your pride and joy, the things you boast in and are proud of. Find joy in them, and be content in them. This is a challenge that may call for a huge attitude adjustment because this reaction is definitely far from our natural response to trials and suffering.

Glory in Christ's covering! Paul says you can glory and be content in your inglorious infirmities because the mightiness of

Christ rests upon you. "Resting upon you" is a beautiful concept that means to dwell in a tent. In other words, God comes and pitches His tent over you. Think about it—Christ abiding on and enshrining you, overshadowing you. He comes to rest upon you, completely covering your infirmity as with a tabernacle, a tent. You will know God's presence and energy, and others too will recognize that God is empowering and enabling you. The strength He imparts to you in your weaknesses gives testimony that He is fortifying you.

Glory in Christ's strength! Amazingly, when we have limitations imposed upon us we tend to do our best work for the Lord. It is then—in weakness—we are the most dependent on Him. And that is reason to glory. The very weakness of our nature is the chosen condition—a precious, priceless condition—under which God can manifest His strength. Your strengthlessness strengthens your hold on God. So, as Paul declared, "glory" in your infirmities because the power of Christ rests upon you!

Witnessing God's Strength in Others

Many biblical personalities illustrate Paul's same resolve when he declared,

> *I take pleasure in infirmities, in reproaches, in needs,*
> *in persecutions, in distresses, for Christ's sake.*
> *For when I am weak, then I am strong*
> (2 Corinthians 12:10).

Here are a few to inspire you.

Samson—Physical ability is a blessing that we may possess, but it can keep us from being more dependent on God. The story of Samson in the Old Testament (Judges 13–16) is a perfect example of a person who tried to live in his own strength. God gave Samson unusual strength and leadership ability. With these God-given abilities, he was to lead the nation of Israel. But Samson squandered and misused this power in personal and selfish indulgences that ultimately allowed his enemies to gain the secret of his power—his uncut hair. So God's foes cut off Samson's hair, gouged out his eyes, and put him in chains in a prison.

In time Samson was put on public display as proof of the strength of his enemies' gods over the strength of the God of the Israelites. In one last effort, the blind Samson, by then in a state of complete weakness and helplessness, asked God to strengthen him one last time. He prayed, "O Lord GOD, remember me, I pray! Strengthen me, I pray, just this once, O God, that I may with one blow take vengeance on the Philistines for my two eyes!...Let me die with the Philistines!" (Judges 16:28).

And God responded. Samson pulled down the pillars supporting the heathen temple where God's mockers were meeting. The result of God's strength empowering Samson in his weakness was that "the dead that he killed at his death were more than he had killed in his life" (Judges 16:30). In his weakness Samson was made strong.

Elisha—Most great leaders begin their careers as lowly followers. Elisha was a farmer plowing a field when God's powerful prophet, Elijah, passed by and commissioned Elisha to join him (1 Kings 19:16–2 Kings 13:20). For many years Elisha traveled in a servant capacity with the great prophet Elijah. In God's timing Elijah was taken to heaven and Elisha was given the role of God's mighty prophet and spokesman to the Israelites. Scripture records that after having waited and served, Elisha performed twice as many miracles as his mentor. In his weakness Elisha was made strong.

Stephen—The early Christian church had a good problem:

Thousands of people were coming to Christ. Clearly and understandably the leaders of the church needed to study God's Word and pray in order to properly lead this fast-growing church. When the need of the many widows came to the leaders' attention, they asked that godly, wise men be chosen to administer food to the poor, the needy, and the widows. Stephen was one of those chosen to be a servant to others (Acts 6:1-6).

In time God took this humble servant, whose job description was to "serve tables," and empowered him to do "great wonders and signs among the people" (verse 8). Eventually Stephen stood helpless and weak before persecutors. He was filled and empowered with the Holy Spirit and strengthened by a vision of Jesus. As he was stoned to death, Stephen was fortified by God. He called on God, saying, "Lord Jesus, receive my spirit....Lord, do not charge them with this sin" (Acts 7:59-60). In his weakness Stephen was made strong.

Do you want to join these servants of God who found their strength in Him? Take a step...or two...or three...forward!

– Taking a Step Forward –

I'm sure you know people who are going through unbearable trials. Do you think, as I thought about Mary, *How do they bear these horrible problems?* Well, we now know that a seemingly impossible situation is precisely what God can use to let His glory and majesty shine. Through our weaknesses, God can receive full credit for what He accomplishes through us. Without His power and enablement, it is impossible to bear challenging experiences in a Christlike manner.

I love the truth of God's strength in our weakness because it means that in Him and because of Him, you and I can boldly step up to—and into—our trials and triumph over every one of them! In most showdowns there is a victor and a victory. Someone wins. We usually don't know in advance who the winner will be. We only know the outcome when the battle is over. But as God's child you get to go into every situation—every battle!—in life *knowing* beforehand that due to God's grace you *will* overcome, you *will* be the victor, you *will* triumph. You *will* never meet any situation where God's power cannot enable you and His grace won't abide with you.

This realization is life changing! Just think: There is nothing that will ever come your way that you cannot handle. There is no trial you will ever face that you cannot manage with God's help. God's strength and power will be there when you need them. Therefore, be bold!

Boldly believe in God's grace and power.

Boldly step into your trials.

Boldly anticipate the greatest victory of all—
God's strength displayed through your
weakness.

*God knows how to balance burdens
and blessings, suffering and glory.*[1]

WARREN WIERSBE

16

Becoming a Work of Art

⁂

I am glad to boast about my weaknesses,
so that the power of Christ may work through me.
Since I know it is all for Christ's good,
I am quite content with my weaknesses and with
insults, hardships, persecutions, and calamities.
For when I am weak, then I am strong.

2 Corinthians 12:10 NLT

My mother grew up during a time when young girls were taught to sew and do needlework. As you can probably guess, I too learned to sew and stitch. At some point in my married life, I decided to cross-stitch a large scene. It was a huge, complicated project that took several years to complete. During those years I carried it with me everywhere. I even took it along on a trip to Israel because of the large amounts of plane time, bus time, and down time between the various points of interest.

As I worked away, many passengers on the flights and those

who were on our tour walked by and shook their heads. Some stopped to ask what I was creating. They wondered because all they could see was the underside of my needlework—a jumbled mess of colored threads that seemed to have no pattern or form. It wasn't until I turned the material over that they could see the beauty and clear image of the scene. Only then could they comprehend the picture and even marvel at what I was trying to accomplish—a work of art.

God's use of trials and tests in our lives is somewhat like my needlework projects. We view our trials from the "underside," the human side, the earthly side. All we see is a mass of unfortunate trials and tragedies that are many times ugly, confusing, and disturbing. But what God wants us to understand is that He is producing works of art. His plans and ways may be unglamorous at times and often contain some pain, but the end results are people of beauty, strength, and grace.

Understanding God's Process

The process God uses to mature us—to transform us into masterpieces—is difficult to grasp. If we had our way, spiritual growth would definitely occur by quick, magical, pain-free means. We would simply wave a wand, and *Voila!* we would be instantly perfect. But that's not the way God chooses to work in us.

The apostle Paul never viewed spiritual growth as an easy process. However, it did take him a while (three rounds of prayer!) to understand that his "thorn in the flesh" (2 Corinthians 12:7) was given to him to mature him to the point where he realized that his weakness provided Christ an opportunity to demonstrate His power in him. Once Paul comprehended that God's "strength is made perfect in weakness" (verse 9), he gave himself over wholeheartedly to God's method and means of working in him. In fact, he gave way to the point where he could with great pleasure boast in his weaknesses and welcome adversities of all kinds. To put it in today's language, Paul said, "Bring it on! Go ahead, give me any and every kind of trial and weakness." He wrote: "I take pleasure in infirmities, in reproaches, in needs, in persecutions, in distresses, for Christ's sake. For when I am weak, then I am strong" (verse 10).

Perfecting Involves Infirmities

Paul listed a handful of conditions and difficulties that he "took pleasure in" because it gave God opportunities to work in his life and the lives of others. First Paul mentions physical "infirmities" (NKJV), "weaknesses" (NIV), "humiliations" (KJV). These terms refer to a literal lack of strength and indicate an inability to produce results.

I've certainly experienced "negative" physical strength, and you probably have too. We've all registered zero—or lower—on the energy scale at some time. For one entire year I was anemic. For the first half of that year I didn't know it. I just kept wondering, *What is wrong with me? I have no energy.* Finally I got the diagnosis of anemia and was put on a treatment plan. Believe me, I know how it feels to have a complete want of strength, to suffer an infirmity.

I also know what it means to experience God's power in my weakness. According to His plan, energy was removed from one area of my life—the physical area. And that put me in a much slower, less-active mode, which led to using my rebuilding time to write, which led to birthing my book *A Woman After God's Own Heart®*, which has sold nearly one million copies, helping women here in the States and many other countries.[1] (God truly blessed my writing as I shared His principles for living.) Not only did I

> *I was a weak vessel through whom God's glorious power and grace could shine all the more brilliantly.*

make it through my personal energy crisis, but I was abundantly empowered with God's energy to be used by Him in a way I had never dreamed of before.

Perhaps the most tired and weak I've ever been (that was not the result of a health problem) was while dealing with our home, possessions, and family in preparation for moving to the mission field. We sold some things, packed some things, stored some things, shipped some things, and moved some things...in addition to attending numerous going-away parties, obtaining passport photos and passports, getting physicals and immunizations, and making sure we had our birth certificates, marriage license, school records for our daughters, and updating and obtaining our health and life insurance. Everything I did for months in a row called for great physical exertion. God's marvelous grace empowered me to make it through!

But His work in me was not over! Little did I realize that God was doing much more than helping me "make it through." He was helping me grow! He stretched me in the marathon of preparations to perfect me for greater ministry on the other side—in Singapore. I grew to the place of being able to sustain and maintain a breakneck, warp-speed, full-on ministry to Singaporean women, in addition to caring for my husband and family in a foreign country.

God proved He would strengthen, enable, and empower me in any and every situation, especially those that weakened me. I was a weak vessel through whom His glorious power and grace could shine all the more brilliantly. I tasted a very tiny bite of what the apostle Paul...and John Wesley...came to know: I experienced God's might. Wesley, the founder of Methodism, reportedly preached 42,000 sermons, traveled 4,500 miles a year, rode horseback (primarily) 60 to 70 miles a day, and preached an average of three sermons a day. At age 83 he wrote, "I am a wonder to myself. I am never tired, either with preaching, writing, or traveling." My own ministry to women was by no means this demanding, but I identify with the realization and wonder of experiencing God-given energy and force!

I'm sure you too have endured weakness and/or tiredness due to illness, excessive physical exertion, or trying times. I'm also sure that as His child you are empowered in countless ways by our faithful God as He works in you to create a work of beauty. Whatever your infirmity is, be confident of this very thing—when you are weak, you are strong…because Christ exhibits *His* strength in your weakness. Count on it. Be content in it. Wonder at it. Enjoy it.

Perfecting Involves Reproaches

Next on Paul's list of hardships and trials in 2 Corinthians 12:10 is "reproaches." These may involve insolence, injury, physical harm, and pain. Such harm can come in the form of insults or ill-treatment. Graduating up the scale, it can include suffering and torture.

In reading biographies of great Christians and martyrs, the women in my book club learned about the many "reproaches" they endured. There was not one thing these sufferers for Christ could do to help themselves or escape as their tormentors caused them pain. But we also learned of the grace, power, and might those believers received from God to endure their mistreatment. The power of Christ "rested" upon them (2 Corinthians 12:9) and spread Himself (His tabernacle, a tent) over them.

Reproaches also include being forsaken by a good friend…or being the target of a calculated and publicly uttered insult meant to harm you…or facing an infuriated crowd…or dealing with an unfair judge in a lawsuit. (Paul, the writer of these words and the creator of this list, certainly had some experience with all of these!) We can thank the Lord He "knows how to balance burdens and blessings, suffering and glory."[2]

Perfecting Involves Needs

Next in 2 Corinthians 12:10 Paul names "necessities." This includes distress and pain, hardships and deprivations. We could say it is when there is not enough—not enough food, not enough money, not enough time.

At one time in my life I even felt like there wasn't enough husband! Jim was attending seminary and working four jobs. And who lived next door? A family in which the husband and father worked for the gas company and rode his bicycle each day the three blocks to and from work. He left for work in the morning at five minutes before eight...and he got home at five minutes after five. That gave him three or four hours in his day to spend time with his wife and kids, paint the house, mow the lawn, plant and take care of his garden, and make knickknacks in his woodworking shop. And my husband? He left at four-thirty in the morning and got home around midnight. We certainly didn't have much time to spend together as a family, our paint was peeling, our lawn went uncut, and there were a lot of other undone "guy" jobs around the homestead. I most certainly felt deprived. There just wasn't enough husband in my life!

I remember reading about Ruth Graham and the fact that at one time her husband, Billy, was gone about ten months a year. In her book of poetry *Sitting by My Laughing Fire*, Ruth wrote about "the close of the door" and how long it would be before that door opened again and her husband walked through it, home at last. But for Ruth and me (and certainly for me to a much lesser degree than Ruth Graham!), there was a necessity God asked us to persevere through to achieve His purposes. God enabled each of us to do His will...and to go without. He taught me, for sure, that it wasn't so bad. After all, I had Him and all His grace and strength and power and might, not to mention His presence to see me through. My daughter Courtney, and her husband, Paul, have four little ones. Paul, a Navy submariner, is out to sea six months at a time. And I hear Courtney parroting my own words, which were parroted from Ruth Graham: "I try to make the most of all that comes and the least of all that goes."

What are you doing without? What is missing from your life? What is there not enough of? Missionary J. Hudson Taylor depended upon God daily for decades to supply funds and food for the many orphans he took care of. Yet he never lost sight of God's faithfulness. He wrote, "In the greatest difficulties, in the heaviest trials, in the deepest poverty and necessities, God has never failed me: The financial balance for the entire China Inland Mission yesterday was twenty-five cents. Praise the Lord! Twenty-five cents...plus all the promises of God."[3]

Friend, lay your hardship, your lack, your great difficulty, your heavy trial, your deep poverty and necessities next to God's every-thingness and "praise the Lord"! You'll quickly discover this truth: All that you need is all that God is and more.

Perfecting Involves Persecutions

The next hardship Paul mentions in 2 Corinthians 12:10 is "persecution," meaning "to be put to flight, or driven away, or driven out of your home." In Old Testament times God's people, the Israelites, were led away from their homes and homeland—the Promised Land!—and put into captivity in foreign lands.

In New Testament times Christians were dispersed as persecution set in and they were driven out or forced to flee for their lives. I have already mentioned Priscilla, a woman in the New Testament who, along with her husband Aquila, was forced to leave their home in Rome (Acts 18:2). Yet God enabled and empowered Priscilla (and Aquila) no matter where she was. Whatever home Priscilla had, she opened and shared with others...including the apostle Paul (verse 3). Apollos, who became a great orator for the cause of Christ, became even more effective after Priscilla and Aquila took him aside and shared their more accurate knowledge (verse 26). I wouldn't be surprised if Aquila and Priscilla did this in their home that they opened for fellowship and church meetings (Romans 16:5)!

Rather than mope and succumb to self-pity, sadness, and resentment because of being forced to move, Priscilla found strength, power, and joy in the Lord to the extent that she was content and shared what she did have with others. The work of God's kingdom was furthered by this dear wife and husband's heart and hospitality.

> *Look to God and leave your situation and its outcome to Him. He has promised He will take care of you... and He will.*

What are you doing without? Who is making your life difficult? Who is bothering you, pursuing you, forcing you in the opposite direction of your dreams? Paul suffered persecution and opposition from the day he believed until the day he died. Yet he never gave in or gave up. He never broke, and he never turned back. Paul counted on God's promise of sufficient grace—and received it. And so can you! Look to God and leave your situation and its outcome to Him. God promised He will take care of you...and He will!

> *Come to Me, all you who labor and are heavy laden, and I will give you rest. Take My yoke upon you and learn from Me, for I am gentle and lowly in heart, and you will find rest for your souls*
> (MATTHEW 11:28-29).

Jesus is the Lord of all power and might, and He will use both to give you shelter in your storms and a place when you are homeless—a home in Him. God's grace and power is sufficient for your every challenge.

Perfecting Involves Distresses

And then there are the "distresses" we face (2 Corinthians 12:10). These can be imposed by external circumstance or inward pressure. They include any kind of anguish, difficulties, and times of stress God asks us to go through. I call this family of challenges the "trials of too much." If "trials of necessities" relate to "trials of too little" (when there is not enough), "distresses" are when there's "too much"—too much pressure, too much stress, too much pain, too much calamity.

Job, in the Old Testament, is definitely an example of suffering the "trials of too much." He lost his family, his land, his possessions, his home, his health, and his reputation. Eventually Job lost everything. How did he handle his "distresses"? Job acknowledged, "The LORD gave, and the LORD has taken away; blessed be the name of the LORD" (Job 1:21).

And the apostle Paul once again provides his own list of "trials of too much." He was in prison often (too much), flogged severely (too much), exposed to death again and again (too much), received 39 lashes (too much), beaten with rods (too much), stoned nearly to death (too much), shipwrecked three times (too much), experienced dangers from rivers (too much), and faced bandits (again, too much)…and that's not all! Paul's list goes on to include much more of "too much" (2 Corinthians 11:23-27)!

What distresses are you experiencing right now? What is your current "trial of too much"? As noted repeatedly, God's grace is sufficient for every distress! He showers you with as much as you need of Him, His power, His strength, and His might to handle all that seems to be too much.

Putting Everything Together

I once read about a man—Thomas Cranmer—who was martyred by the Catholic Queen Mary because he was a Protestant. Her reign began the persecutions of Christians at Oxford, England, which led to this man having to watch two of his converts (Ridley and Latimer) die in the very flames he was soon to enter. These three men suffered all of the maladies mentioned by Paul—infirmities, reproaches, needs, persecutions, and distresses. The three of them had met before their deaths and encouraged each other to "be of good heart, for God will either assuage the fire, the flame, or else strengthen us to abide it."

For them it was the latter: *In* the fire God gave them His strength in their weakness and at their time of need, at their weakest point. As the first two perished, they cried out, "For Christ's sake, more fire!" They never wavered. Then it was Cranmer's turn to die in the fire. The fiery stake highlighted the truth he had written some years earlier:

> I have learned from experience that God never shines forth more brightly and puts out the beams of His mercy and consolation or a strength and firmness of spirit more clearly or impressively upon the minds of His people than when they are under the most extreme pain and distress, both of mind and body, that He may then, more especially, show Himself to be the God of His people when He seems to have altogether forsaken them, then glorifying them, when He is thought to be destroying them.[4]

God's power and grace extends to you today, just as it did to Paul...and the many others mentioned in this chapter. You too may say along with Paul, "When I am weak, then I am strong." Your varied weaknesses make you strong in Christ. And when you are the weakest is when you are actually the strongest of all because you have the strength of Christ manifest in you. Therefore, as writer and speaker Jill Briscoe exhorts, "Hang your weakness upon His strength."

The words to this hymn by Annie Flint put Paul's teaching together in poetry. They also show us how God creates a work of art!

He Giveth More Grace

He giveth more grace as our burdens grow greater,
He sendeth more strength as our labors increase;
To added afflictions He addeth His mercy,
To multiplied trials He multiplies peace.

When we have exhausted our store of endurance,
When our strength has failed ere the day is half
    done,
When we reach the end of our hoarded resources
Our Father's full giving is only begun.

His love has no limits, His grace has no measure,
His power no boundary known unto men;
For out of His infinite riches in Jesus
He giveth, and giveth, and giveth again.[5]

—Taking a Step Forward—

God's path through your trials is truly a wonder, isn't it? Here are some additional steps to help get you through every difficulty.

Step 1: Know. Especially know these facts about God: His grace is sufficient and His strength is made perfect in your weakness.

Step 2: Grow. Spiritual growth and endurance is yours when you trust in God's power and grace and count on them in every difficulty.

Step 3: Go. Whatever comes your way, go through it. And know you will go through many "its" of life. Keep on keeping on! Don't look for an easy way out. Realize that God keeps His children up spiritually when they are down physically and facing other problems (such as deprivation, persecution...and the rest of Paul's list). The weight of trials is what gives your feet spiritual traction.

Step 4: Show. Take pleasure in showing off God's strength. Be glad when you suffer because the power of Christ rests upon you and shows forth His mighty power through your weaknesses and needs.

Section 5

Becoming an Enduring Woman

*Every temptation is an opportunity for us
to draw nearer to God.*[1]

GEORGE SWEETING

17

Enduring Difficult Times

⅊

*No temptation has overtaken you except such
as is common to man; but God is faithful, who will
not allow you to be tempted beyond what you are
able, but with the temptation will also make the way
of escape, that you may be able to bear it.*

1 Corinthians 10:13

According to author Tim Hansel, several research scientists wrote a book after studying 413 famous and exceptionally gifted people. Their goal was to learn what had produced such lives. From the very beginning of the study the patterns that emerged were startling. For instance, 7 out of 10 of these gifted persons came from homes that were in no way warm and peaceful. Instead they were homes riddled with trauma—such as missing or argumentative parents, poverty, and people with physical handicaps.[2]

This book of results presents revealing insights into the roots of people who were later called "great." Amazingly, almost every conceivable handicap was successfully overcome by these eminent people. Virtually all of them had triumphed over severe difficulties.

Well, you and I have difficulties too. As we've been discussing, these problems give us opportunities to know the power of God and who we are in Him…and what we really can be and do with His help. Going through difficulties gives us endurance, which is the ability to hold up under and remain in our trials until they're over.

Examining Trials and Temptations

First Corinthians 10:13 gives us a little different perspective on our trials than we've seen so far. Paul is writing to the Corinthian church and using the 40-year wandering in the wilderness of the children of Israel to illustrate what happens when God's people give in to trials. After pointing out the Israelites' special standing with God and the many miracles they witnessed, Paul cites a list of their sins (verses 1-10). Paul then says, "Now all these things happened to them as examples, and they were written for our admonition, upon whom the ends of the ages have come. Therefore let him who thinks he stands take heed lest he fall" (verses 11-12). After the warning, Paul gives God's perspective to understanding and dealing with our trials:

> No temptation has overtaken you except such as is common to man; but God is faithful, who will not allow you to be tempted beyond what you are able, but with the temptation will also make the way of escape, that you may be able to bear it (1 Corinthians 10:13).

This verse uses the word *temptation* instead of *trial*. However, it is the same Greek word translated "trial" used in James 1:2 and 1 Peter 4:12. Some Bible scholars explain the difference in the translation of this word this way: "trials" denotes outward issues such as tragedy, oppression, distresses, the things the apostle Paul speaks of in his own life (2 Corinthians 12:10). "Temptation" refers to the inward pressures to succumb to sin such as the example of the Israelites' sinfulness.[3]

Paul is saying that the external trials of thirst, hunger, heat, lack of a home, lack of stability, and so forth that the Israelites experienced led to the internal temptation to complain, murmer, argue, and question, which ultimately led them to rebel against God and His servant, Moses.

Therefore, as I have noted throughout this book, trials and tests—which now include "temptations"—are not to be seen as bad or evil things. They are simply opportunities for us to "endure pressure from an external source" (which the Bible calls a trial) or from an internal issue (which in 1 Corinthians 10:13 is seen as a temptation). In either case, how well we respond and then endure reaffirms and strengthens our faith and trust in God.

From this point on, when I refer to tests, trials, and temptations I'm actually referring to the same thing—trials!

Accepting Temptation

Endurance begins with acknowledging and accepting that trials will come. This helps us to not fall apart on the front end of a trial. I'm sure you've probably heard this quip: "We are born, we pay taxes, and then we die." These are facts of life. And trials are too!

❧ The writer of the book of James said: "My brethren, count it all joy when you fall into various trials" (James 1:2).

❧ The apostle Peter said: "Beloved, do not think it strange concerning the fiery trial which is to try you, as though some strange thing happened to you" (1 Peter 4:12).

❧ The apostle Paul said: "No temptation has overtaken you except such as is common to man; but God is faithful, who will not allow you to be tempted beyond what you are able, but with the temptation will also make the way of escape, that you may be able to bear it" (1 Corinthians 10:13).

Responding to Temptation

To me, this upfront knowledge of the reality of trials causes a great deal of sober mindedness. Temptations will come...and they come with purpose. They are designed to test us so that we emerge from them stronger than ever, with a greater ability to endure what is to come. Trials are not meant to break us, and they are neutral. Only when we give in to a temptation does our action become sin. So we need to ask, "How am I going to handle trials? What am I to do when they come?"

I'm sure you can recall times when people you know...or even you...have responded poorly to temptations:

We can be crybabies when trials come along. (Trust me, I have been.)

We can be brats (and, yes, I have also been this) and have fits when trials come.

We can act like teenagers and go into sullen, sour moods when confronted with difficulties. (And, yes, I'm well acquainted with this option as well!)

But how about adults? When an adult doesn't get what he or she wants, what happens? A mature, sober-minded woman will not cry, will not throw a fit, will not sulk. No, she won't be a crybaby or a brat or a moody juvenile. Why would she act like that when she knows trials will come, that trials are part of life?

So the first piece of advice for enduring trials and difficult times—*be knowledgeable*. God is reminding us again that trials will come.

Preparing for Temptation

Knowing that trials will come motivates us to prepare for them. If you know you will be facing that problem again tomorrow... and on another day...and even another day, *plan* out how you will face it! One way to do this is picture it like scenes we see often on TV newscasts: The police, or FBI, or Alcohol, Tobacco, and Firearms forces are in a standoff. They surround the site of an illegal operation. They are alert, armed, in position. All day long they crouch on the ground watching, their shields up, their weaponry ready. They know trouble is coming.

Like these officers who were certain trouble was looming on the horizon, we need to be on guard, armed, shields ready, watchful, prepared for trouble. We know trials are coming! We know trouble is around the corner. We should never be surprised or ill-prepared when it arrives. There is no reason to ever be caught off guard, to be shaken, to be blown away by difficulties.

> *We need to be alert, watching, waiting, on guard at all times for the trials that will surely come.*

My husband spent several decades in the U.S. Army Reserves. Once a year he left home to go somewhere for two weeks of active training. One year his unit was shipped to Minnesota in the dead of winter to learn how to set up a portable hospital in snowy, frigid conditions. When he returned home and unloaded his duffle bag, he had a handful of brown plastic packages. They looked and felt like they had books in them, but inside were dehydrated food rations. Every day when his unit went out, they were sent with their meal packet—Meals Ready to Eat (MRE)—complete with lots of Tabasco sauce because evidently they didn't taste very good! These soldiers went out ready for the day's needs, and they even carried extras in case there was an emergency or a blizzard and they couldn't get back to base.

The army sent their soldiers out with an ample supply of food and other necessities every day just in case. Unlike some skiers, hikers, and climbers I read about every year who go for a day outing in the mountains that surround our home in Washington State and end up stranded in a surprise storm for days or a week, Jim was prepared and equipped for the worst. You and I need to think and plan ahead, knowing trials will come.

Do you remember your driver's training or driver's education class...or the classes your children took? Potential drivers are taught to drive defensively. The slogan is: "Look out for the other driver!" We need to follow this advice and be alert, watching, waiting, on guard at all times for the trials that will surely come.

I recently came back from a family reunion where I listened to my brother Robert talk about his oldest child. She had just gotten her driver's license. Robert was at a dinner party when his insurance agent said, "Well now, Robert, when she gets in her first wreck, here's what you need to tell her to do....When that wreck happens, be sure you call me. When that wreck occurs, make sure you have this information."

Robert replied, "Wait a minute! What do you mean *when that wreck happens?*"

"Oh, it's coming," his agent friend said as he laughed.

And of course it did!

Take a cue from this scene. Trials will come. And we need to be knowledgeable about what to do *when* they arrive. If we fail to prepare before the "wreck" happens, we'll suffer even more because we won't know what to do, how to protect ourselves, how to get help, or how to help the other person.

Like the Boy Scouts' motto says: "Be prepared."

Planning for Temptation

If you know company is coming, do you prepare? If you're like me and many of my friends, you get out your best recipes, make a grocery list, and go to the store to get all the ingredients for some great meals. Then you change the sheets on the guest-room bed. Next you clean the bathroom. And if you have time you even do an overall massive cleaning!

Or if you're going on vacation, what do you do? You wash and pack the clothes you'll need, call the newspaper office to stop daily delivery, and arrange for a neighbor to bring in your mail and feed the cat. You write checks for your bills and make sure they're in the mail before you leave. You get the house tidy and shut down, water any houseplants, and take care of the lawn. You're ready to leave home.

To prepare for anything—whether a vacation, a hike, a houseguest...or trials—planning is a key help. Let's suppose you look at today's date on your calendar and written across it in bold red letters are these words: *Trial coming!* or *Trial—3:00 PM.* What would you do if it was that clear a trial was coming? Answer: You would prepare for it.

> *We can't be prepared for everything in our humanness, but we can be ready by keeping close to the Lord.*

Jim taught a seminar for college students at our church on setting lifetime goals. One question each student was to answer was, "If you knew you would be struck dead by lightning six months from today, how would you spend the next six months of your life?" One girl was brave enough to show me her answer. She wrote, "I would spend the whole six months on my knees praying and witnessing to others about Christ."

A question like Jim asked really brings us back to the reality of what truly counts. So take a look at your own life and evaluate how prepared you are for what is coming...the things you know and even the things you're not sure of. For instance, you know your husband is coming home after work and he'll probably need some downtime, some dinner, some company, some loving support. And when your kids get home from school they'll want to tell you about their day, eat, perhaps share their troubles, and have some fun. And at some time you, someone in your family, or a friend will get sick—maybe with a cold, maybe with something worse. What can you do to be ready for the medical expenses, the time needed for caring for the sick person, the support he or she will need? And what about the mundane expenses of appliances and vehicles that break down? And then there are the major trials, the tragedies of deaths, accidents, emergencies, and so forth.

We can't be prepared for everything in our humanness, but we can be ready by keeping close to the Lord.

To begin, get into God's Word. Where do you think your boldness and confidence and power will come from when you face your sure-to-come trials and temptations? From God's powerful Word! Be faithful in prayer. Prayer is how and where you acknowledge your weaknesses and tell God about your need for Him. And it's how and where your faith to endure tests will be fortified. And prayer is how you stay connected to God and ask for His strength, His wisdom, His grace, His mercy, and His endurance.

Staying Positive

We can stay positive as we prepare for and face tests and temptations because God is with us:

❧ He promises you will be able to bear your trials and resist any temptation to give in to sin (1 Corinthians 10:13).

❧ He promises you will come out on the other side of your trials with more patience (James 1:3).

❧ He promises you will be perfect and whole, lacking nothing when your testing is over (James 1:4).

To approach your trials with anything other than a positive attitude is to poke a hole in your energy bucket. You need all your energy to deal with your trials and temptations, so keep your "bucket" and faith in good shape. Don't become negative or embittered toward the people who are involved in your trials. Grudges, resentment, and bitterness short-circuit the growth process and lead to failure, which often results in the temptation to sin.

And maintain a positive attitude toward God. He knows all about the trials coming your way. To successfully handle your tests, remember God is your hope. He is your salvation. He is your rock. He is the ultimate supplier of strength and power, of wisdom and endurance. *He* is what you need! Don't jeopardize your relationship with Him and your victory in your trials by becoming bitter or resentful. If you give in to this temptation, you will become paralyzed, unable to rightly respond and endure and succeed.

The prophet Jeremiah is a classic study of one who endured. For years he was faithful to deliver God's messages to a sinful people...and no one listened! On top of that, Jeremiah's life was often threatened. Perhaps his endurance was drawn from the encouraging words God spoke to him before sending him on his preaching ministry: "Do not be afraid of their faces, for I am with you to deliver you" (Jeremiah 19:8). Jeremiah did become discouraged and disappointed that the people wouldn't obey God, but he never wavered in his obedience to his calling. He remained steadfast in his trials...for 40 years!

You and I are called to endure too. We are to hold up under pressure, put up with difficult people, events, and circumstances, tolerate injustice and unfair treatment, and remain in our trials for as long as they continue...even for life if God calls us to that.

—Taking a Step Forward—

Tim Hansel, in writing his book *You've Gotta Keep Dancin'*, observed that perhaps one of the most commonly used sentences in the English language is: *If I can just get through this problem, then everything will be all right.*

He goes on to say the birth of maturity is when we realize that once we get through our present problem, there will be another one slightly larger and a little more intense waiting to take its place. If we are to grow up and grow in Christ, Tim says the time must come when we make this realization.

Let's take a giant step right now! You and I can decide not to go into a negative tailspin every time a trial comes. After all, we know a trial will come, and then another one, and another one, and another one. We also know that God is generous and loving and will give us the strength, encouragement, and wisdom to endure and overcome any adversity. I'm ready. Are you?

We can never have a temptation that has not been experienced by millions of other people. Circumstances differ but basic temptations do not.[1]

John MacArthur Jr.

18

There Is Nothing New Under the Sun

֍

*No temptation has overtaken you but such as is
common to man; and God is faithful, who will not
allow you to be tempted beyond what you are able,
but with the temptation will provide the way of
escape also, so that you will be able to endure it.*

1 Corinthians 10:13 NASB

֍ Some years, months, weeks, days, and even hours we feel
overwhelmed with the trials we have and the ones we know
are coming. For example, picture this real-life, seven-day episode
in a woman's life—in my life to be exact!

To start things off, my two daughters were home from
college for spring break. But it wasn't spring break for me.
And my church didn't suspend the women's classes and
Bible studies for Easter the following weekend, which meant
I was scheduled to teach four times at church. I agonized,

Why, oh why, can't my daughters have the same spring break dates everyone else around here has? But no, they had their week off during this one overloaded, odd-ball week. And believe me, the party atmosphere was definitely reigning in our home! *How can I possibly get my studying and preparations done?* I fretted.

In addition, that particular week I had a huge deadline to meet. And it was something I'd never done before. I was writing my first book proposal and the two chapters required to accompany it! The week prior I sat in a library carrel for two days and nights doing research and telling myself, "I'm not afraid of hard work. I can do this. Others have done this before me. I'm not afraid of hard work. God will help me!" And now I *really* needed His help!

Plus a short time before my daughters' spring break, a woman whose daughter was having an affair, leaving her husband, and taking her child with her called. She wanted to know if I would spend the day with her daughter if she could get her daughter to fly out to my area. This would happen on Tuesday…two days after my daughters left and the day before Wednesday when I teach the women's Bible study. I began praying, "Oh Lord, on Tuesday? Really?" I felt God wanted me to meet with this woman, and it would surely be a tough counseling session. I said yes.

Another call I received was from a woman in my church who was married to an unbeliever. This dear soul wore sunglasses to class Sunday because her husband had beaten her. She wanted to know how I…or the church…could help her with her situation—her trials.

Then I had run into a lady after church. Her daughter was divorcing her husband, and the concerned mom wanted to know, "Are there any books or CDs or advice you could give me to pass on to my daughter? Can you give me a list?"

(Ah, the telephone! You know the sound—and the scene! Ding-a-ling-a-ling. Ding-a-ling-a-ling. Every time the phone rings, it's usually a request to bring God's help to someone who is facing trials...which can easily translate into a trial for me as well. I'm sure you can relate!)

Even the demands and responsibilities of the week beyond this one were already hanging over me. My husband and I had to make a lot of financial decisions. (Remember, spring and Easter time also means tax time!) Taxes were due soon, and we had to get everything ready for our tax appointment on Thursday.

I was also involved in a huge, five-day pastors' conference. The preparations for the wives' meetings during the conference called for hours on the phone getting that organized.

And...and...and...

These tests represented only a portion of what I was waking up to every day during that particular time. My heart was racing, and my thoughts were going right along with it, screaming, "Trials coming! Trials coming!"

I'll share how I survived this nightmare week in chapter 20, but for now let's explore how to successfully handle the many trials we women face every day, every week, every month.

What's a Woman to Do?

I know your list of trials looks just as overwhelming as mine. So what are we to do? How can we handle life's many issues in a mature way? How can we walk through our multiple challenges without falling apart? We explored God's first answer for walking through life's trials in the preceding chapter: *We understand and accept that trials and temptations will come...and keep on coming*

(1 Corinthians 10:13). They are never going to let up. (And I want to add that this fact sure makes heaven look inviting!)

And now we can look at another truth from 1 Corinthians 10:13:

> No temptation has overtaken you except such as is common to man; but God is faithful, who will not allow you to be tempted beyond what you are able, but with the temptation will also make the way of escape, that you may be able to bear it.

God's second message to us is: *We realize that our trials are in no way unique.* Others have gone through whatever is in front of us. People have experienced this before…and made it through successfully God's way. It's like nineteenth-century English Bishop Joseph Lightfoot said when his driver stopped the carriage and suggested Lightfoot would be safer to walk because of the narrowness of a mountain pass. "Other carriages must have taken this road. Drive on," Lightfoot responded.

Nothing Is Unique

First Corinthians 10:13 tells us in no uncertain terms that no temptation has overtaken us that hasn't happened to others. No believer is exempt from trials, and no trial is unique. All trials are common, usual—typical, not exceptional. They are no different from what other people experience. To quote one scholarly source, "We can never have a temptation that has not been experienced by millions of other people. Circumstances differ but basic temptations do not."[2] This is an encouragement! It reminds us that success is possible. No temptation is beyond human resistance. Any and all temptations we ever face *can* be endured! We are not facing super-human, freakish trials. Our trials have been resisted and endured by God's grace to His people through the centuries.

Right now as I think through the week I described earlier in this chapter, I can still recall my anxiety. *Wow!* That one week looked like an impossible-to-cross mountain range. But studying this truth to teach a class called "Finding God's Path Through Trials" gave me courage and the assurance that I wasn't alone. I knew I could make it through because others had. I realized the overly busy week packed with more responsibilities than I thought I had time and energy for was not unique to me and, in fact, was completely common!

The same is true for all of our problems. Divorce, separation, strain in marriage, an alcoholic husband, a child with needs, loss of a loved one, widowhood, and so forth may be first-time experiences for an individual, but God says they are common to mankind. Physical affliction, infertility, menopause, a declining parent, sickness, cancer treatments, and terminal illness happen to people all the time. Unfortunately, that's life. Our problems are simply human problems. People handle them, grow through them, triumph over them, and endure them.

Hearing God's Good News

Is there any good news regarding our trials? Absolutely! Because our tests and temptations are common, they can be endured *if* and *when* we remain firm under the adversity and resist the temptation to sin in our situation. No cracks, no weaknesses, no giving-in allowed! We can endure! We can bear up without yielding to the flesh. So no crybabies, brats, or moody women allowed. We can be mature women who endure our surprises and hardships so that we grow stronger in the Lord.

Unfortunately I, like you, meet a lot of women who fail to grow in endurance because they have a distorted, unbiblical view of their problems. They withdraw from life or find others in their predicament and huddle with them around the difficulties, moaning and groaning and commiserating. Don't get me wrong. There is certainly a place and a time for mutual support and encouragement.

We are to come alongside others with empathy and comfort. God commands it and expects it of us. And—a bonus!—our suffering helps us minister to others because we can share our experience and growth as we relate to them:

> Blessed be the God and Father of our Lord Jesus Christ, the Father of mercies and God of all comfort, who comforts us in all our tribulation, that we may be able to comfort those who are in any trouble, with the comfort with which we ourselves are comforted by God (2 Corinthians 1:3-4).

But we must admit, we have a natural tendency to group together and dwell on a problem, seeking sympathy. But God's good news? Because our problems are common, we can endure as we go—and grow—through them.

For instance, I was asked to teach a class on Sundays for women married to unbelievers. For years these brave women met weekly to pray and talk about their "unique" situation…and their husbands. On Day One I announced we were going to do a Bible study on the women in the Bible and the scriptures directed toward wives—all wives! The Bible speaks to *all* wives in *all* situations. These dear women were Christian wives, first and foremost, who happened to be married to unbelievers. So the focus of the group was tweaked away from their situations and onto their roles as wives—their assignments from God—and on God's grace. Of course, we were careful to apply biblical truths we learned to real-life situations. But emphasis was first placed on the truths of the Bible to us as individuals.

In another instance, a woman came to sign up for the church's mentoring ministry. When I asked if she would like to be in this group or that group or another group, based on the day of the week she was free to meet and the part of town she lived in, she said, "Oh no! I can't be in a group. I'm different. I'm not average like the other women. I have special issues. You don't understand. I have to have someone mentor me one-on-one because my situation is different." Yes, you know what I was thinking: "No temptation has overtaken you except such as is *common* to man."

At one time, in the course of teaching through the book of Proverbs, our class came to a lesson on sex centered around "the wise wife" from the book of Proverbs, chapter 5 (especially verses 15-20). Later I heard that one wife in the class had come up with ten reasons why she couldn't apply the wisdom of these scriptures. In fact, her reasons extended to include reasons why God would never expect her to apply these teachings to her life. In her mind she was different, she was the unique woman on the planet who didn't have to follow God's Word in this area.

> *We have to fight our tendency to build our problems up, even to the point of taking pride in them. We can't let ourselves think and act like we are different, unique, set apart, special when it comes to trials.*

Many women come to me for advice regarding their situations. They first share their problems and then ask me for help. So I start giving them a little guidance…and then it comes. I hope it won't happen. I pray it won't happen: "Please, Lord, just this once!" But I soon hear the words again, those two little words: "Yes, but…" followed by "my situation is different. My circumstances are unusual. Let me tell you why that won't work in my case."

I gently explain, "No, there is nothing in any woman's life that is not common. God has written the entire Bible, His complete, revealed, God-breathed Word, to spell out His counsel and speak to all of our common problems. He has not left anyone without help. Indeed, His instruction is the best help we have! He has given us everything that pertains to life and to living it in a godly manner. That's what 2 Peter 1:3 tells us. God also says there is nothing new under the sun (Ecclesiastes 1:9). No new perversions, abuses, sins, problems, or issues. There is nothing new.

If we want to be healthy and open to God's guidance, we need to accept this truth that *all* our problems are common. We have to fight our tendency to build our problems up, even to the point of taking pride in them. We cannot allow ourselves to think and act like we are different, unique, set apart, special when it comes to trials and temptations. The danger is that we will soon decide certain scriptures don't apply to us because of our uniqueness. Or even worse, we may gradually conclude that God would never expect us to follow His commands in certain areas.

Yes, many of the trials we encounter are terrible and traumatic. But God informs us they are still "common." We're like everybody else when it comes to problems. God's Word has been given to us, and it includes advice for handling *everything* that can ever happen to any person in a lifetime—including you.

Handling Problems God's Way

At one time I attended a class called "A Study in Submission." Each time our group met we spent the first hour studying a portion of the book of Esther and the second hour applying what the text had shown us about a lifestyle of submission. We covered not only wives following their husbands' leadership, but submission in its many forms in the body of Christ.

One woman, however, decided she was exempt from following her husband because he wasn't a Christian. She was looking for loopholes in God's instruction.

Yet in the same class there was another woman—also married to an unbeliever—who announced she was taking the class to be sure she was being the best wife she could be to her husband.

She wanted to do a better job—she wanted to do her best! This gallant wife was not going to allow her circumstances to interfere with her understanding and implementing of biblical truth. She wanted to endure—even excel!—in her situation and grow spiritually.

And my hat also goes off to a woman in my college Bible study. She talked with me about her parents, who had just gotten a divorce. To add insult upon injury, her dad had quickly remarried. This woman said, "Hey, I know others have gone through this. I'm getting as much advice as I can. I'm asking everybody for help. I want to go through this in the right way."

What a refreshing attitude!

Once we refuse to buy the lie that we're facing unique circumstances, trials, experiences, or temptations, we can find comfort in the universality of our situation. We find assurance that we can endure because it is common and others have gone through it. Others have come out successfully on the other side. And if we acknowledge that all trials are "common to man," we can readily accept that God's Word holds the answers to our dilemmas and is the balm for our souls.

—Taking a Step Forward—

A primary ingredient in being a mature woman in Christ is to desire endurance. And to get endurance, we must face and go through trials. One of my daughters clipped a cartoon from the Sunday paper. A single woman was having a little fit with her boyfriend. She sat down on the couch all alone after he left in desperation because he just couldn't understand her. Her words were something like, "Well, sometimes a woman just wants to be a girl."

Isn't that so true? Sometimes we just want to be a big crybaby or a big brat. We want to throw a fit or sulk. But biblically we don't have that luxury because as mature women we want to grow in the Lord and in life. After all, we have husbands, families, friends, careers, and ministries to attend to. The stakes are simply too high to refuse to seek what God is teaching us and building in us.

> *Because trials are common, you are not alone in your struggles. Others have gone before you.*

Do you want to be an enduring woman? To be a woman who can undergo hardship or difficulty without faltering, without giving in, without breaking? Then you have to *want* it. I share with women almost weekly that desire is critical to spiritual growth and maturity. Yes, we can know what the Bible says. We can even know how to *do* what the Bible says. But if we don't *desire to do* what the Bible says, we won't. It's as simple as that. If you truly want to be an enduring woman who grows and matures spiritually and in every other facet of life, you will be. It's your choice.

Dear reader, please understand that because trials are common, *you are not alone* in your struggles. Others have gone before you. What can you do?

Step 1: Read your Bible. More specifically, look at the common sufferings endured by God's people in biblical times. Begin with the life of Christ, your Savior. The Bible says, "We do not have a High Priest who cannot sympathize with our weaknesses, but was in all points tempted as we are, yet without sin" (Hebrews 4:15). Reading the four gospels will show you how Jesus handled every temptation known to humanity.

Also acquaint yourself with the women of the Bible. For every problem you face there is a woman in the Bible who has probably faced it too. And if you don't find your specific problem in their struggles, you will find a woman who had to deal with the underlying principle or who experienced the same emotions, feelings, concerns, and challenges you are.

Get to really know the lives of the Bible's heroes. There isn't enough space in this book to share what men like Abraham, Moses, David, and the disciples endured by God's grace and through faith in Him. Those who have gone before us serve as examples, and their stories are preserved by God for our admonition (1 Corinthians 10:11).

Step 2: Read Christian biographies. The life stories of God's many saints through the ages will show you how they endured their trials. You will see how common suffering is. Biography after biography tells of endurance and triumph and lasting impact for Christ. You will never be the same after witnessing how others endured their difficult situations.

Step 3: Request advice from those who have suffered. Catalog the experiences of others. Find out how they held on and triumphed in their problems. I always ask, "Did you have a certain scripture that was most meaningful to you in your situation?" Hebrews 4:12 tell us "the word of God is living and powerful." Each verse anyone shares with you or that you read can be placed in your arsenal for fighting your own trials and facing your own temptations. They give you something to hang on to, to use as a weapon, to think about, and to help you endure your trials in the right way—God's way!

Step 4: Reach out for help from others. Ask for help. This is hard for many people, but do it. I struggled with a certain parenting trial for two years before I asked anyone for help. I thought no one had been through what I was facing. But as the situation worsened, I finally prayed and asked God to direct me to women who might have advice and wisdom to share. As a result, I sought help from four different women. And their first response to my problem? Each one of them laughed out loud. They said, "Oh, it's your turn! Every parent has this problem. We've all had this problem. Here's what you do..." *Whew!* I wasn't alone any longer. I was normal. My problem was normal. There was hope. And there's hope for you too in whatever trial you are facing right now!

The assurances of this verse [1 Corinthians 10:13] is a permanent comfort and source of strength to believers. Our trust is in the faithfulness of God.[1]

19

Trusting in God's Faithfulness

❦

*No temptation has seized you except what is
common to man. And God is faithful; he will not let
you be tempted beyond what you can bear. But when
you are tempted, he will also provide a way out so
that you can stand up under it.*

1 Corinthians 10:13 NIV

When I purchased my first Bible (as an adult woman with a husband and two children), a fishbowl filled with highlighter pens was next to the Christian bookstore's cash register. On a whim I reached in and selected two of them. The first one was pink. As a new woman in Christ, I was also a new wife in Christ, as well as a new mom in Christ. In my mind and heart I chose "female" pink and purposed to begin the next morning reading through my new Bible. I planned to look for and mark all the passages I found that taught about being a godly woman, wife, mother, and homemaker. I wish you could see my Bible all these years later! Not only did God's many "pink passages" guide me in my daily life and relationships, but the knowledge they have given me has blessed others as I have shared with women the truths I found.

The second highlighter I selected was yellow-gold. This was going to be my "God" marker, and I couldn't think of a better color than gold for Him! With that pen in hand, I prayed, "Oh God, I am the new girl on the block—Your new child. I want to know You—all about You!" The next day when I started reading God's Word at Genesis 1:1, I began marking all the "gold passages" in the Bible too, all the verses that tell facts about God, focus on His attributes, reveal how He works in the lives of His people through the ages, and share the many promises He gives to believers.

Focusing on God's Faithfulness

I probably don't need to tell you that the verse for this section of our book on finding God's path through our trials is marked in gold in my Bible. Hear the Word of the Lord...about Himself!

> No temptation has overtaken you except such as is common to man; but God is faithful, who will not allow you to be tempted beyond what you are able, but with the temptation will also make the way of escape, that you may be able to bear it (1 Corinthians 10:13).

God's faithfulness is a resource for us when our own faithfulness is tested.

"But God is faithful." *Wow!* How refreshing—and stabilizing—this fact is as we continue our study on trials, tests, and temptations. We already know that trials will come...and keep on coming. But now we learn another fact: God is faithful...and will keep on being faithful! When it comes to you and your tests and trials, you can find hope in the fact that the same God who designs and oversees your tests also knows your limits. He knows all about you—your weaknesses and limitations and your future needs for spiritual strength, stamina, and endurance. His faithfulness will allow you to endure everything that comes your way.

This truth of God's faithfulness means "no believer can claim that he was overwhelmed by temptation or that 'the devil made me do it.' No one, not even Satan, can make us sin….No temptation is inherently stronger than our spiritual resources. People sin because they willingly sin."[2]

And speaking of resources, we have God's faithfulness as a resource when our faithfulness is tested in a trial or temptation. Our trust is to be in God and His faithfulness, not our own.

Counting on God's Faithful Keeping

As you face your sure-to-come difficulties, consider these golden facts about God and His power to keep and care for you. You can count on Him!

- God will "keep" you in all your ways (Psalm 91:11).

- God will "keep" what you have committed to Him (2 Timothy 1:12).

- God will "keep" you as a shepherd cares for His flock (Jeremiah 31:10).

- God will "keep" you in His perfect peace (Isaiah 26:3).

- God will "keep" you from falling away from Him (Jude 24).

- God will "keep" you during the hour of your temptation and support you in the time of your trials (1 Corinthians 10:13).

Truly God's care of you is complete. It covers you when you are helpless, in trouble, in tribulation, in testing, and in every other condition. And the coverage is day and night!

Counting on God's Perfect Timing

God's faithfulness is perfect in its timing:

❧ *In salvation*—"In due time Christ died for the ungodly" (Romans 5:6). God's Son, the Lord Jesus Christ, died at the correct, precise, predetermined point in history to effect salvation for all.

❧ *In daily conflict*—Because our times are in God's hands, we say along with the psalmist, "Deliver me from the hand of my enemies, and from those who persecute me" (Psalm 31:15).

❧ *In daily life*—God has "appointed [a] time for everything. And there is a time for every event under heaven" (Ecclesiastes 3:1 NASB). Due to God's sovereign oversight of the days of your life, no event in your entire lifespan is left to chance. God's perfect timing encompasses every day, every season, and every event you will ever encounter or need to endure.

Counting on God's Provision

God promises that no temptation you ever come up against will ever be more than you can bear. He also promises that *if* a temptation becomes too much for you, He will create a way through and out of it for you. And He knows exactly when to provide the way of escape (1 Corinthians 10:13).

That's what God did for His people (Exodus 14). The Egyptian pharaoh's army was pursuing the Israelites to bring them back into slavery. The former slaves ran for their lives...until they came up against the Red Sea. With no human way out of their predicament, God made a way for His beloved people to escape from the hostile forces. He miraculously parted the Red Sea! His people walked across dry land while the waters stood like walls on the sides of their path. And then God just as miraculously caused the waters to come together again as Pharaoh's army chased the Israelites on the sea floor! Needless to say, the Egyptian army drowned.

Counting on God's Perfect Knowledge

God alone knows perfectly what we can and cannot bear. He also knows that each test or temptation teaches us lessons we need for growing spiritually and gaining greater endurance. He also knows when enough is enough. And when we reach that point, He graciously provides all we need to be victors in our trials, to pass through and endure them without sinning, without giving in to temptation.

I love this story that beautifully illustrates the confidence we can have in God. A saint from another era wrote of a customer in a shop where a small boy stood with outstretched arms while the owner placed package after package from the shelves into the boy's waiting arms. As the pile grew higher and higher and the weight increased, the customer could stand it no longer. He remarked to the boy, "My lad, you'll never be able to carry all that!" Turning around, the boy replied with a smile, "My father knows how much I can carry." Such assurance and trust! Just think, your heavenly Father knows exactly how much you can carry!

And what about when we wonder if we can withstand the tests? Daniel's three friends, Shadrach, Meshach and Abed-nego, completely relied on God's protection and knowledge...and God, as always, fulfilled His promises. Although the fire the three Hebrews endured was heated to seven times its normal heat, God preserved and delivered them. Previously these three true worshipers had declared to King Nebuchadnezzar, "Our God whom we serve is able to deliver us from the burning fiery furnace, and He will deliver us from your hand, O king. But if not, let it be known to you, O king, that we do not serve your gods, nor will we worship the gold image which you have set up" (Daniel 3:17-18). These faithful men were willing to die before they would give in to temptation. May this be true of us as well!

Counting on God's Perfect Compassion

The prophet Jeremiah wrote of God's faithfulness. As we learned earlier, Jeremiah preached God's message for 40 years. And yet he saw no fruit from his preaching. In fact, he experienced physical and emotional suffering as the people turned on him with wrath and disdain and murderous intent. Nevertheless, in the midst of his affliction and suffering, Jeremiah found hope in God's faithfulness. The only light in Jeremiah's life was the knowledge of God's past faithfulness and the assurance of His promise of continued faithfulness in the future. Jeremiah wrote these words of bright hope for today and strength for tomorrow:

> Through the LORD's mercies we are not consumed, because His compassions fail not. They are new every morning; great is Your faithfulness. "The LORD is my portion," says my soul, "therefore I hope in Him!" (Lamentations 3:22-24).

Many of the great hymns of faith were written as a result of dramatic experiences, such as a salvation experience or special awareness of God's presence and grace at a time of great sorrow or loss. The wonderful hymn "Great Is Thy Faithfulness" by Thomas O. Chisholm was written out of a full heart as a simple testimony of God's never-failing compassion and mercy. As Mr. Chisholm reflected on God's moment by moment, "morning by morning" personal faithfulness to him, a man who lived 94 years, he couldn't contain his emotions. The result? A treasured hymn extolling God's forever faithfulness and unchanging character. The next time you are at a church, pick up a hymnal and let Mr. Chisholm's beautiful words remind you again of God's faithfulness to you.

Counting on God's Faithfulness

When I first taught the material in this book to a group of women at my church, I referred to thinking on the truths in the Bible as "spiritual mental health." I wanted to share some of the scriptural truths that had been especially helpful to me in my own journey of discovering God's path through my trials. First Corinthians 10:13, the "no temptation has overcome you" verse, was one of the scriptures I chose to include in that class.

Why is this gem from all of Scripture one of my spiritual mental health verses? Because it taught me to stop thinking and saying, "I'm not going to make it" or "I can't do this" whenever I came up against a trial. Instead this verse helped me think and say, "I am going to make it. I can do this because God is faithful and will make sure of it...if I count on Him, do my part, and hang in there to see it through!"

This verse is a promise, a truth, a fact. God promises no trial will ever be more than I can bear, more than I can endure by His grace and in His power.

> *My role in each trial is to remain faithful to God and follow through with action. I am to love Him, to trust Him, to call upon His resources.*

He also reveals a truth and a fact about Himself: "God is faithful." So I have a choice to make each time I bump against a trial or temptation. I can think faulty thoughts—lies!—about how I'm not going to make it through or can't make it through. Or I can think healthy thoughts—God's truths!—that believe and accept that He is indeed faithful, that He promises He will see me through my problem...which means I *can* make it through! God also promises my trials will not be more than I can endure, and if they get close to that point, He promises He will come to my rescue and show me a way out or through the trial so I can make it. Trusting God's faithfulness is the path through every trial, and it is also the path to spiritual maturity.

My role in each trial is to remain faithful to God and follow through with action. I am to love Him, to trust Him, to count on His resources, to fight against temptation, to ask Him to enable me to endure through the pain, sorrow, heartache, deprivation, life-threatening situations, and to resist coming up with my own solutions to my trials. When I do this, I discover His faithful help for my every need.

—Taking a Step Forward—

God's faithfulness. What a divine resource! And it is available to all His children. So what can you do in the shadow of something so awesome? A really big step you can take is to reflect on God's faithfulness to you just as songwriter Thomas Chisholm did. Whatever issue you're facing today, whether it is a medical diagnosis or treatment, a physical limitation, a loss in your family, a difficult situation with a spouse or child or friend, a lack of finances...remember: "God is faithful" (1 Corinthians 10:13).

You and I (and everyone else) are forgetful people. So it helps to purposefully and willfully remember that God has never failed to be faithful. Actively remember how He has "kept" you in the past. Remember how He has protected you and your family from times of serious harm. And wonder of wonders, remember how His timing has always been perfect. At the precise moment when you seemed to be at the end of your rope, God orchestrated a deliverance, a solution, an answer to your prayer, a way of escape from a temptation, or the opening of a path through it.

Please don't forget God's goodness and mercy and unfailing compassion.

Remember, they are new *every* morning and fill your *every* day (Lamentations 3:22-23)!

> ❧ Remind yourself regularly of the faithfulness of God to you, His dear child.

> ❧ Recall God's moment by moment, morning by morning faithfulness to you.

> ❧ Record the evidence you have personally witnessed of the unfailing faithfulness of our covenant-keeping God and the many wonderful displays of His providing care.

> ❧ Rely on Him in every trying situation.

The mode of [God's] deliverance shall be ready simultaneously with the temptation....
The way to escape is different in different temptations, but for each temptation God [will] provide the special means of escaping it.[1]

20

Triumphing over Temptation

ૐ

The temptations that come into your life
are no different from what others experience.
And God is faithful.
He will keep the temptation from becoming so strong
that you can't stand up against it.
When you are tempted, he will show you a way out
so that you will not give in to it.

1 Corinthians 10:13 NLT

ૐ When I think of the faithfulness of God, I am utterly overwhelmed. Not only does God call us and save us, but He
also superintends every detail of our lives...including the temptations and trials that come our way. On top of that, He is faithful
to guide us each step of the way *through* our trials.

As we've learned—and acknowledged—in our study about
testing and temptations, we are weak. There is no doubt about it!
We are finite, ordinary, human vessels of flesh and bone, formed

from the dust of the ground. Is this cause to rejoice? The apostle Paul gloried in his infirmities. Remember? He explained, "When I am weak, then I am strong" due to the power of Christ (2 Corinthians 12:9-10).

I like this observation by pioneer missionary Hudson Taylor, founder of China Inland Mission: "All God's giants have been weak men and women who did great things for God because they counted on His faithfulness." I'm sure Hudson Taylor read and reread the apostle Paul's reminder of the faithfulness of God in 1 Corinthians 10:13 before penning this remark. Let us also be reminded of God's faithfulness in assisting us to triumph over temptation:

> No temptation has overtaken you except such as is common to man; but God is faithful, who will not allow you to be tempted beyond what you are able, but with the temptation will also make the way of escape, that you may be able to bear it (1 Corinthians 10:13).

Do you want to do great things for God and His people? Do you want to exhibit His power and might, His love and grace to others? Do you want to bring Him honor and glory? Then trust in Him. Count on His faithfulness.

Factoring in God's Faithfulness

We now know *our trials are common*. Any and every temptation or trial we face is typical—not exceptional, not unique. We also know that *God is faithful* to us in our trials. He is not a mere spectator. And He never leaves us alone to fend for ourselves or muddle through on our own. Instead God shows us two distinct ways He proves and shows His faithfulness.

Promise #1—God will make sure you are never overwhelmed

by temptation. Paul assures you, "God is faithful, who will not allow you to be tempted beyond what you are able" to bear. God will not allow any test to become so strong that you, His dear child, cannot stand up against it.

Think about these "greats" who discovered God's faithfulness to help them endure their trials and temptations:

> *Imagine the myriad times God has stepped in to provide comfort, hope, and encouragement to His people. And He does this for you too!*

Shadrach, Meshach, and Abed-nego were tested by God in a fiery furnace (see Daniel 3). You've met this terrific trio several times before in this book, but in their test we dramatically witness God enabling them to triumph over temptation. God gave them the strength, faith, grace, and companionship they needed to endure the temptation to save their lives by denying Him and bowing down to a heathen king and his golden idol. In fact He (or one of His angels) joined them in the fire (verse 25)!

Jesus was tested in the wilderness (see Matthew 4:1-11). For 40 days and nights the righteous, sinless Son of God was left alone without food to be tested by Satan. But as soon as Jesus had endured the test, the Father immediately sent His angels to give food, water, strength, companionship, and encouragement to His Son.

Jesus also agonized in the garden of Gethsemane as He faced death on a cross (Luke 22). The Scripture says, "And being in agony, [Jesus] prayed more earnestly. Then His sweat became like great drops of blood falling down to the ground" (verse 44). Yet God let His Son face and endure what was coming. The Bible does tell us that "an angel appeared to Him from heaven, strengthening

Him" (verse 43). God did not deliver Jesus from the cross but He did supply Jesus with all He needed to endure.

Stephen faced death by stoning (Acts 7). Yet the Bible reports that Stephen, "being full of the Holy Spirit, gazed into heaven and saw the glory of God, and Jesus standing at the right hand of God" (verse 55). God left His faithful servant and martyr in his situation. Stephen did die and it was not a pleasant death. But God gave him exactly what he needed to endure it—in this case, a vision of Himself and His Son. Stephen said, "Look! I see the heavens opened and the Son of Man standing at the right hand of God!" (verse 56). What an amazing, gracious thing for God to do!

And these are but a few examples of God's faithfulness in giving His grace and strength to His children in their difficult situations. Imagine the myriad times God has stepped in to provide comfort and hope and encouragement to His people. And He gives these things at the very moment they are needed to keep people from being overwhelmed by any temptation or trial. And He does this for you too!

Promise #2—God will make a way for you to escape or show you a way through your trials. This is His promise to you and me. God doesn't keep us from being tempted, but He does, *with* the temptation, ensure that we can bear it by enabling us to stand up under the pressure of the trial or by giving us an escape route.

In using the words "the way of escape," Paul is conveying the idea of a ship that is about to be dashed on the rocks but suddenly a narrow passage is sighted and the boat reaches a safe shore (1 Corinthians 10:13). Or imagine an army trapped in a valley by another army. While on the verge of annihilation, an opening is spotted through the mountains. The army flees through it and is saved to fight another day under better conditions.

Our role is to stay in our trials. God's role is to help us endure them or to get us out of them. He knows all about our trials, about how much we can endure, about the path ahead, about our limits. God is the author of the test...and the controller of the test as well. And He is the finisher of it too.

And guess what? God is also the deliverer from the test! This means we can go into any test and *know* we can handle it, we can endure it, we can remain faithful to God through it because He remains faithful to us. When we get into a situation, we have but one godly choice—to stay in it and endure it.

Then we do what I call "waiting for the miracle." We wait to see how God will deliver us. We go into every situation knowing He can—and He will—because "the Lord knows how to deliver the godly out of temptations" (2 Peter 2:9). So all we need to do is stay in the trials, resist sin, and wait to see how God chooses to work in our lives through our situation.

Two Women in Trials

Meet a woman who couldn't "wait for the miracle" while suffering in her trial of barrenness. You've met her before—her name was Sarah, and her story spans Genesis 11:31–23:2. Sarah simply couldn't wait to have a baby, especially after she heard God promise a son to her and her husband. As year after year of hope and heartache passed by, Sarah finally gave up on God and took the situation into her own hands. She connived until she figured out a way to get what she wanted. She had a great idea—Abraham, her husband, could have a baby with her maid! Then when the babe was born, Sarah and Abraham would consider it theirs. So Sarah manipulated others (her husband and her maid) and implemented her grand scheme. Sure enough, Ishmael was born to Abraham by Sarah's servant, Hagar. Unfortunately, the rest of the situation didn't pan out like Sarah hoped.

However, God did, of course, follow through on His promise. Sarah did get her miracle. When she was 90 years old—way

> *Getting His people through or out of hard situations is God's job. Nobody can do it perfectly except Him.*

past child-bearing age!—she gave birth to a son and heir. Yes, Sarah did finally get her baby, whom she named Isaac, but she also got a great deal of trouble because of her interference. Strife reigned between her son and the son borne by her maid. The feud between the two boys is still raging today in the tension between the two nations that resulted from Sarah's impatience: the Jews (Isaac) and the Arabs (Ishmael).

Elizabeth, on the other hand, waited on God for her miracle. (Her story is recorded in Luke 1.) She too was childless and beyond childbearing age. She too suffered. But she did not scheme and use others to get what she longed for. Instead she waited. Hear God's description of Elizabeth's character and lifestyle while waiting and going without her dream: "And they [Zacharias and Elizabeth] were both righteous before God, walking in all the commandments and ordinances of the Lord, blameless" (verse 6). No crybaby, no brat, no moody person here! Also no devious plans hatched or people duped! It's simple: You cannot be righteous and blameless and walking in all the commandments and ordinances of the Lord while acting with such immaturity. And so Elizabeth waited...and experienced the miracle of childbirth in her old age.

Getting His people through or out of hard situations is God's job. Nobody can do it perfectly except Him. Our tendency is to help ourselves out of a problem by helping God out a little. We lie, we cancel commitments, we avoid events or people or situations, we manipulate.

Letting God Work

In chapter 18 I shared my personal list of trials I was facing in the week to come, including counseling a wife planning to leave her husband, celebrating and spending time with my daughters on their spring break, preparing for teaching opportunities during Easter, writing a book proposal and the first two chapters of the book itself by a certain time, helping a wife whose husband struck her, getting ready for tax season, and on and on. These are great opportunities for ministry...but the timing was a huge problem. Well, here's how my week worked out. Correction—Here's how *God* worked out my week!

The woman who wanted to leave her husband and was flying in from Chicago for counseling on Tuesday (remember, it had to be on Tuesday!) didn't come. Her heart was so hardened she didn't want any advice from anybody. So God gave me Tuesday back. He made the way for me to escape. I'd been sitting on the edge of panic, frantically thinking, "I've got to call and tell this lady I can't do this!" I was tempted to take the situation into my own hands, to work it all out to suit me...or to work my own way out of it. But after prayer and sensing the seriousness of her need, consulting with and getting my husband's hearty approval, I decided, "No, I'll make myself available and see what God does. It will be a joy to be used by Him...but He's got to work it all out!"

Then there was the young married woman whose husband hit her. We set up the appointment six weeks in advance, and yet every morning I whined, "Oh, Jim, I've got to call this lady. I've got to cancel. There's just no way I am going to have time to..." Then I realized I was working on creating my own way of escape. I was jumping ship! So I calmed myself before the Lord, and said, "No, I'm going to honor the appointment and see what God does. He's got to work this out." Well, not only did this young wife not come, she never even called me to say what happened or why she didn't come. (This is why I do my mentoring at home. I can work right up to the minute the doorbell rings. I'm not wasting time sitting in a restaurant or a park waiting for someone who might not show.) I tried later to reach her, but she had left town. So I did the best—actually the greatest!—thing I could do. I prayed for her and her husband.

In these instances I fought against my original decisions. Yet with God's help and through prayer I did not succumb to the temptation to cancel, or get myself out of my commitments, or take things into my own hands. Instead I endured through them—or at least was willing to endure through them. But God was faithful. He provided grace for me to meet my many other commitments and responsibilities...and He provided the way to escape for me when needed in these two cases.

But I also know that had I spent Tuesday with the woman from Chicago and met with the other woman who needed help, God would have supplied the grace for me to be faithful *and* get all my obligations for that particular week taken care of.

Oh, dear friend, this is our God! The more we see God work (like I did in my hectic week!), the more we trust Him. And the more of His faithfulness we experience, the more we can endure. We surprise ourselves with our new levels of stamina as we continue to function in spite of our trials and hold out in our situations regardless of the pain. To God be the glory!

–Taking a Step Forward –

Think again about the many truths in 1 Corinthians 10:13: "No temptation has overtaken you except such as is common to man;

but God is faithful, who will not allow you to be tempted beyond what you are able, but with the temptation will also make the way of escape, that you may be able to bear it." Surely such a golden verse from God requires responses from our hearts!

What should you and I do and not do? Choose what step—or steps—you will take to become an enduring woman, one who triumphs through her trials and temptations...all the way to the end. God's goal for you is that you hold up under pressure, put up with difficult people, events, or circumstances, and remain firm in your trials while waiting on His faithfulness.

Don't...

...be shocked

...be discouraged

...think you're the only one to suffer or have short-comings.

Do...

...realize your weaknesses

...turn to God for help in resisting temptation.

Do count on God's faithfulness to...

...assist you in facing your problems and remaining strong in them

...keep your problems from becoming more than you can endure

...protect you from unbearable temptations

...make ways for you to escape if situations become unbearable.

Don't forget to do your part in your trials. You are to...

...exhibit self-discipline

...recognize the people and situations that tempt you to sin

...run from all that is wrong

...choose to do only what is right

...seek friends who love God and will help you when you're tempted

...pray for God's help.

A Final Word

Be careful for nothing.
Be prayerful for everything.
Be thankful for anything.[1]

21

Gaining Something Grand

*Be anxious for nothing, but in everything by
prayer and supplication, with thanksgiving, let your
requests be made known to God.*

Philippians 4:6

In a University of Wisconsin study on what people worry about, statisticians were astonished by these interesting results:

- 40 percent were apprehensive over things that had never happened

- 30 percent were overly concerned with past matters that were now beyond their control—gone, over with, and already behind them

- 12 percent were anxiously fearful of the future loss of their health (although their only illness was in their active imaginations)

- 18 percent were busy worrying about family,

friends, and neighbors with no basis whatsoever for their fears

❧ *Total:* 100 percent worried about nothing![2]

What percentage group would you land in if this doctor had enrolled you in his group of worriers? (And you wouldn't be alone!) Worrying is a common malady, especially for women. That's understandable on the surface because we have so many responsibilities. Our lists of things to do and people to care for usually seems endless. And besides our obligations and the people we tend to, we can't forget those pesky trials and temptations that are always hovering around us.

So how can we deal with worry—especially as it relates to our trials...the ones we face now and the ones that will come in the future?

Recapping Our Journey

You and I have been moving along on a journey through the issue of trials to better understand how to find God's path through them. So far we've learned to accept our trials with joy *when* (not if) they come—to be joyful women. We've gained greater understanding about what it means to become a stable woman who stays in her trials and develops perseverance. We've also discovered how to be more mature and accept trials as a way to grow spiritually and develop greater endurance.

The final frontier for us is securing peace of mind and heart as we walk through our stress-producing trials, problems, and difficulties. How can we become peaceful women who take whatever comes our way without losing it—without losing our temper, our dignity, our grip, our minds?

Handling All Your Trials

Through the apostle Paul God gives us the answer: *Pray!* In Philippians 4:6 we read:

Be anxious for nothing, but in everything by prayer
and supplication, with thanksgiving, let your requests
be made known to God.

In just one verse Paul gives you and me a simple-but-all-inclusive, two-pronged answer for dealing with all our trials. His advice comes in two commands. The first command is negative, the second is positive.

First, the negative. Paul, a man with extensive, personal experience with trials, tests, temptations, and tribulations, first tells us there is something we are to do: We are not to worry...period. "Be anxious for nothing," he wrote. It's hard to miss this direct message! I especially like the Bible translation that says, "Don't worry about anything" (NLT)!

In other words, we are to take no thought of anything that would lead us to worry. We are not to even think such things. We are not to even think about thinking about it!

And isn't this what Jesus told us? He said we are not to be anxious about clothes, or about food, or about our lifespan. Furthermore, we are not to be anxious about persecution, or about tomorrow, or about what we would say if we were brought to trial before unbelieving tormentors (Matthew 6:25-34; 10:19).

But Paul goes a step further and adds, "Don't be anxious about anything." There are no boundaries. No, you aren't to worry about your job...or your health...or whatever. The command is "Do not worry!"

How can we tell we are anxious? How does anxiety show its ugly head?

We question. Just imagine a little fretful hand-wringing going on as you race through your day. "Oh, what am I going to do? Where is this trial or problem going? How is this going to end... and what if it never ends?" We are full of question after question: "What will people think? Can I get it all done? Will there be enough money? Enough time? Enough energy?" These questions and worries reveal a lack of trust in God. Paul says, "Stop it! No worrying allowed."

We are obsessed. We have a knack for taking something small and giving it an inordinate amount of thought and attention. We are masters at obsessing. No matter what we're doing, our thoughts seem to return again and again to minuscule matters. It's almost as if we can't think about anything else.

We are consumed. Our time and energy are taken up by something that occurred in the past...or some trial that has never actually occurred but might! As a result we are not able to function effectively. Whatever we are worrying about owns us and ruins day after day after day.

> *There is nothing—no trial, no test, no temptation— so great you cannot bring it to the Lord, to the Creator of the heavens and the earth.*

We are distracted. We can't focus on life's real issues because we are unable to concentrate. We are plagued with an inability to focus. Sure, we may go through the motions of daily living, but we are drawn away from successfully handling reality because of worry.

What are we women anxious about? If we're married, we love to worry about our husbands. And if we have children, there's even more to worry about! And if we're not married, well, that's another concern. And then there are finances, health, the well-being of our family members, challenges at work, and...and...and... Oh, our worry list just keeps expanding!

And what about the future? Since we never know what's around the corner, we can always wonder...and worry about it. Eek! We also worry about relationships and friendships, especially those that are awkward or tension filled. We worry about our nation, politics, and war. The list of fears could go on forever. And yet we hear Paul reminding us not to worry about anything.

Next, the positive. In Philippians 4:6 Paul tells us that instead of worrying and being anxious, we are to *do* something positive. We are to pray! "In everything by prayer and supplication, with thanksgiving, let your requests be made known to God."

In case you were worrying about what you were going to do if you couldn't worry, now you have God's answer! "Be anxious for *nothing,* but in *everything*" be praying. God's solution for all your worries and fears is to pray...in and about everything. You're to pray in and under all circumstances!

God makes it easy for you. You only need to remember one thing: The way to worry about nothing is to be praying about everything. There is nothing—no trial, no test, no temptation—so great that you cannot bring it to the Lord, to the Creator of the heavens and the earth. He is more than able to help you handle everything. He supplies you with complete peace of mind and heart (verse 7). And there is no bother or trial too small to take to Him because He cares for *all* your concerns (1 Peter 5:7). And here's a news flash: If your care is too small to be turned over to God in prayer, that care is also too small to worry about.

Comprehending the Breadth of Prayer

Did you notice Paul mentioned four elements of prayer...or four kinds of prayer? Each is a weapon to be used to conquer your fears and worries when you encounter and endure trials, hardships, and suffering.

Prayer—Bringing any and all of your needs to God. This is

as simple as bowing your head and talking to God. Paul and the elders of Ephesus practiced this kind of prayer when Paul was leaving them to travel to Jerusalem. After teaching, Paul "knelt down and prayed with them all" (Acts 20:36).

Supplication—Appealing to God or entreating Him. This kind of prayer focuses on and includes more details about your needs… and a prayer list helps. If there is a trial that's bothering you, put it on a prayer list. Then take it to God. Hannah did that. Being barren, she prayed specifically for a male child (1 Samuel 1:10-11). Covering your Number One concern in prayer first thing in the morning takes care of the majority of your worries for the day. And what a day that will turn out to be!

Thanksgiving—Recalling God's goodness and mercy. Expressing gratitude to God is a cheerful way to manage the trials in your life and, at the same time, fulfill God's command—"In everything give thanks" (1 Thessalonians 5:18). Being thankful guards your heart against bitterness. It keeps you from failing to forgive others. It also cultivates graciousness in your character, developing an attitude of gratitude.

If you are faithful to give thanks, you won't be complaining because you can't be grateful and complaining at the same time! You also won't be murmuring or griping. You won't be sour, bitter, or negative. And here's a bonus! You won't be a troublemaker either. So follow the psalmist's example of praying to God with thanksgiving: "It is good to give thanks to the LORD, and to sing praises to Your name, O Most High; to declare Your lovingkindness in the morning, and Your faithfulness every night" (Psalm 92:1-2).

Requests—Presenting definite, precise petitions to the Lord concerning your needs. You can make requests of God based on His character and promises. Note how King Hezekiah acknowledged God's character and attributes when presenting this request:

O LORD God of Israel, the One who dwells between the cherubim, You are God, You alone, of all the kingdoms of the earth. You have made heaven and earth. Incline Your ear, O LORD, and hear; open Your eyes, O LORD, and see.... O LORD our God, I pray, save us from [Sennacherib's] hand, that all the kingdoms of the earth may know that You are the LORD God, You alone (2 Kings 19:15-16,19).

Now, how can you deal with worry? How can you live a worry-free life? How can you handle all the trials of life? Answer: Don't worry about anything. In everything, by prayer, supplication, thanksgiving, and through requests, praise God and ask Him for His help, His answers, His wisdom, His strength, His grace, His provision...His everything (Philippians 4:6)!

And then a miracle will occur! Once you do things God's way—pray instead of worry—you receive something grand. You receive the peace of God that surpasses all understanding. His peace will guard your heart and mind through Christ Jesus (verse 7). In spite of your trials, you will have the peace of God *in* your trials! And the wonderful thing about His peace is that it is immediate. Isn't prayer a marvelous resource from God for dealing with the trials and tribulations of life?

—Taking a Step Forward —

Throughout this book we've focused on the trials that are sure to come our way every day. James instructed us to "count it all joy when you fall into various trials" (James 1:2). Yet James also prescribed prayer as the ultimate solution to handling trials. He counseled, "If any of you lacks wisdom, let him ask of God, who gives to all liberally and without reproach, and it will be given to him" (verse 5).

Paul also prayed. He did what came naturally when he suffered his "thorn in the flesh" (2 Corinthians 12:7). He "pleaded with the Lord three times that it might depart" (verse 8).

So what is your next step on God's path through your trials? It's obvious, isn't it? You must pray!

❧ When you step out and pray you guard your mind from thinking unhealthy thoughts.

❧ When you step out and pray you're producing the cure for all your anxiety.

❧ When you step out and pray you're acknowledging your dependence on the all-powerful God and His resources.

❧ When you step out and pray you're being obedient to the Lord's commands.

❧ When you step out and pray you're ready to experience the peace of God that passes all understanding.

❧ When you step out and pray you can be sure you're on God's path through your trial!

Praying through your trials and adversity forces your roots deeper into the fertile soil of God's love and provision. That's because prayer is the way to ask God for His strength so you can withstand the storms life inevitably brings. Trials are painful, exhausting, burdensome, and bothersome. At times you won't be sure you can carry on. But it is during these dark times that true faith shines the brightest. Believe Jesus' promise that He will never leave you or forsake you (Hebrews 13:5). Take courage, child of the King! And remember, as God's child you are...

❧ ...the most triumphant when most tempted,

❧ ...the most glorious when most afflicted,

❧ ...the most in the favor of God when least in man's;

❧ as your conflicts, so your conquests;

❧ as your tribulations, so your triumphs.[2]

Notes

Chapter 1—Accepting the Truth

1. Albert M. Wells, Jr., comp., *Inspiring Quotations—Contemporary & Classical* (Nashville: Thomas Nelson Publishers, 1982), p. 209.

Chapter 2—Using an Easy Sorting System

1. Elon Foster, *6000 Sermon Illustrations* (Grand Rapids, MI: Baker Book House, 1952/1992), p. 634.

Chapter 3—Evaluating What's Happening

1. Charles F. Pfeiffer and Everett F. Harrison, *The Wycliffe Bible Commentary* (Chicago: Moody Press, 1973), p. 875.

Chapter 4—Expecting Bumps, Roadblocks, and Dead Ends

1. Elisabeth Kübler-Ross, M.D., proposed these now famous five stages of grief in her book *On Death and Dying* (New York: Simon & Schuster/Touchstone, 1969).
2. Tim Hansel, *You Gotta Keep Dancin'* (Colorado Springs: Chariot Victor Publishing/Cook Ministries, 1998), pp. 54-55.

Chapter 5—Looking for Blessings

1. Bruce B. Barton, David R. Veerman, and Neil Wilson, *Life Application Bible Commentary—James* (Wheaton, IL: Tyndale House Publishers, Inc., 1992), p. 7.

Chapter 7—Strengthening Your Staying Power

1. William Barclay, *Letters of James and Peter,* rev. ed. (Philadelphia: Westminster Press, 1976), p. 43.
2. Bruce B. Barton, David R. Veerman, and Neil Wilson, *Life Application Bible Commentary—James* (Wheaton, IL: Tyndale House Publishers, Inc., 1992), p. 7.

Chapter 8—Standing with the Giants of Faith

1. Katherine Workman, quoted in Wells, *Inspiring Quotations—Contemporary & Classical,* p. 69.

Chapter 9—Crossing over to Greatness

1. *Our Daily Bread,* September 1, year unknown.

Chapter 10—Making Decisions that Develop Greatness

1. *Our Daily Bread,* September 1, year unknown.

Chapter 12—Experiencing God's Power and Perfection

1. Kenneth S. Wuest, *Wuest Word Studies from the Greek New Testament,* vol. 3 (Grand Rapids, MI: Wm. B. Eerdmans Publishing Co., 1973), p. 103.
2. See Matthew 27:45,51-53; 28:7; Ephesians 1:7.
3. Ray Beeson and Ranelda Mack Hunsicker *The Hidden Price of Greatness* (Wheaton, IL: Tyndale House Publishers, Inc., 1991), pp. 15-24.

Chapter 13—Finding Strength in God's Grace

1. D.L. Moody, Notes from My Bible and Thoughts from My Library (Grand Rapids, MI: Baker Book House, 1979), p. 289.
2. Adelaide A. Pollard (1862–1934), hymn lyrics, "Have Thine Own Way, Lord," public domain, 1907.
3. Bruce B. Barton, Life Application Bible Commentary—1 & 2 Corinthians (Wheaton, IL: Tyndale House Publishers, Inc., 1999), p. 451.
4. A. Naismith, A Treasury of Notes, Quotes, and Anecdotes (Grand Rapids, MI: Baker Book House, 1976), p. 98.

Chapter 14—Counting on God's Power

1. See Elizabeth George, A Woman After God's Own Heart® and A Mom After God's Own Heart (Eugene, OR: Harvest House Publishers, 1997/2006 and 2005, respectively).
2. Elon Foster, 6000 Sermon Illustrations (Grand Rapids, MI: Baker Book House, 1992), p. 658.
3. Charles Caldwell Ryrie, The Ryrie Study Bible (Chicago: Moody Press, 1978), p. 1766.

Chapter 16—Becoming a Work of Art

1. Warren W. Wiersbe, Be Encouraged (Colorado Springs: Chariot Victor Publishing, 1984), p. 141.
2. See Elizabeth George, A Woman After God's Own Heart® (Eugene OR: Harvest House Publishers, 1997/2006).
3. Wiersbe, Be Encouraged, p. 141.
4. Roy B. Zuck, The Speaker's Quote Book (Grand Rapids, MI: Kregel Publications, 1997), p. 169.
5. John W. Cowart, quoting Thomas Cranmer in People Whose Faith Got Them into Trouble (Downers Grove, IL: InterVarsity Press, 1990), p. 64.
6. Annie Johnson Flint (1866–1932), hymn, "He Giveth More Grace," Orchard Park, New York, in the "Casterline Card" series, number 5510, nd.

Chapter 17—Enduring Difficult Times

1. Lila Empson, Checklist for Life—The Ultimate Handbook (Nashville: Thomas Nelson Publishers, Inc., 2002), p. 103.
2. Tim Hansel cites Victor and Mildred Goertzel, Cradles of Eminence (New York: Little, Brown, & Co., 1962).
3. W.E. Vine, An Expository Dictionary of New Testament Words (Old Tappan, NJ: Fleming H. Revell Co., 1966), p. 117.

Chapter 18—There Is Nothing New Under the Sun

1. John MacArthur Jr., The MacArthur New Testament Commentary—1 Corinthians (Chicago: Moody Press, 1984), p. 228.
2. Ibid., p. 228.

Chapter 19—Trusting in God's Faithfulness

1. Leon Morris, The Tyndale New Testament Commentaries—The First Epistle of Paul to the Corinthians (Grand Rapids, MI: Wm. B. Eerdmans Publishing Company, 1976), p. 144.
2. John MacArthur Jr., The MacArthur New Testament Commentary—1 Corinthians (Chicago: Moody Press, 1984), p. 229.

Chapter 20—Triumphing over Temptation

1. H.D.M. Spence and Joseph S. Exell, The Pulpit Commentary—Vol. 19, Corinthians (Grand Rapids MI: Wm. B. Eerdmans Publishing Co., 1978), p. 324.

Chapter 21—Gaining Something Grand

1. D.L. Moody, Notes from My Bible and Thoughts from My Library (Grand Rapids, MI: Baker Book House, 1979), p. 172.
2. Adapted from Roy B. Zuck, The Speaker's Quote Book (Grand Rapids, MI: Kregel Publications, 1997), p.424.

Acknowledgments

As always, thank you to my dear husband, Jim George, M.Div., Th.M., for your able assistance, guidance, suggestions, and loving encouragement on this project.

I would also like to give a special thanks to the following Editorial team members at Harvest House for their support and work: LaRae Weikert, editorial managing director; Steve Miller, senior editor; and Barbara Gordon, editor. Each of these dear people is a cherished friend as well as a co-laborer in most of my projects.

I also wish to acknowledge the entire staff at Harvest House Publishers—beginning with its president, Bob Hawkins Jr., and including the people in Administration, Editorial, Marketing, Sales, Order Fulfillment, Production, Design & Layout, Distribution, Finance, Information Technologies, and Human Resources—for their support and help in sharing God's Word and wisdom. I appreciate their contributions to my books and ministry.

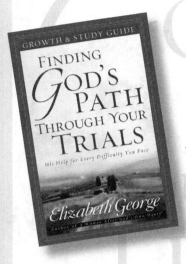

Personal Notes

Personal Notes

Personal Notes

Personal Notes

Personal Notes

Personal Notes

Personal Notes

Personal Notes

Personal Notes

Personal Notes

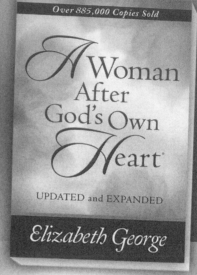

A Woman After God's Own Heart® Study Series

Bible Studies for Busy Women

*God wrote the Bible to change hearts and lives. Every study in this series
is written with that in mind—and is especially focused on helping
Christian women know how God desires for them to live."*

—Elizabeth George

Sharing wisdom gleaned from more than 20 years as a women's Bible study teacher, Elizabeth has prepared insightful lessons that can be completed in 15 to 20 minutes per day. Each lesson includes thought-provoking questions, insights, Bible-study tips, instructions for leading a discussion group, and a "heart response" section to make the Bible passage more personal.

Living with Passion and Purpose
LUKE
Elizabeth George
978-0-7369-0816-0

Becoming a Woman of Beauty & Strength
ESTHER
Elizabeth George
978-0-7369-0489-6

Putting On a Gentle & Quiet Spirit
1 PETER
Elizabeth George
978-0-7369-0290-8

Discovering the Treasures of a Godly Woman
PROVERBS 31
Elizabeth George
978-0-7369-0818-4

Nurturing a Heart of Humility
CHARACTER STUDIES MARY
Elizabeth George
978-0-7369-0300-4

Walking in God's Promises
CHARACTER STUDIES SARAH
Elizabeth George
978-0-7369-0301-1

Experiencing God's Peace
PHILIPPIANS
Elizabeth George
978-0-7369-0209-2

Pursuing Godliness
1 TIMOTHY
Elizabeth George
978-0-7369-0565-4

Cultivating a Life of Character
JUDGES/RUTH
Elizabeth George
978-0-7369-0496-8

Growing in Wisdom & Faith
JAMES
Elizabeth George
978-0-7369-0490-2

HARVEST HOUSE
PUBLISHERS
EUGENE, OREGON 97402
www.harvesthousepublishers.com

Loving God with All Your Mind

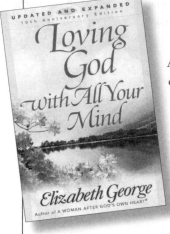

Are you frustrated, worried, or depressed? Are you unsure of what to do in a specific circumstance? Are you wondering if God is in charge? No matter where you are or what your situation is, God knows all about it and is with you! And the more you know Him, the more hope, encouragement, and peace you'll have. Join noted Bible teacher Elizabeth George as she explores six powerful scripture passages that will help you …

❧ grasp God's purpose for life…and move toward it

❧ trust the Lord in all things…even those you don't understand

❧ think on what is true or real…about God and about your life

❧ live one day at a time…without worry or anxiety

❧ navigate the maze of life…successfully

Offering biblical wisdom and personal experience, Elizabeth helps you handle daily life, hard-to-understand situations, and difficult emotions. She invites you to draw closer to God and realize His grace and love in your life!

Life Management for Busy Women

Are you forever falling behind?

Do you long for life to be simpler and more focused?

Are you wondering what your purpose in life is…or if you missed it?

You're not alone! Author Elizabeth George, a busy woman herself, can identify completely. Through the years she has looked to God's Word for answers about a woman's priorities and purposes in life…and how to fit it all in. *Life Management for Busy Women* highlights…

❧ God's guidelines for managing the 7 major areas of life, including spiritual, financial, physical, and relationships

❧ practical disciplines for managing your life more efficiently and effectively

❧ how-to ideas for improving your scheduled and life right away.

As you follow God's plan for making the most of your time, you'll come to know the beauty, simplicity, and power of a life lived according to God's principles and purposes.

The Remarkable Women of the Bible

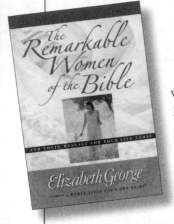

Come and see how God enabled ordinary women to live extraordinary lives! How did He do it? By turning their weaknesses into strengths, their sorrows into joys, and their despair into hope.

Along the way you'll learn great truths about God...

␭ From Eve you'll see God is faithful even when you fail

␭ From Sarah you'll find God always keeps His promises

␭ From Rebekah you'll discover God has a plan for your life

What made these women—and many others—so remarkable? They loved God passionately, looked to Him in life's daily challenges, and yielded to His transforming grace. And you can enjoy God's miraculous work in your life today...by following in their footsteps!

Books by Elizabeth George

- Beautiful in God's Eyes
- Finding God's Path Through Your Trials
- Life Management for Busy Women
- Loving God with All Your Mind
- A Mom After God's Own Heart
- Powerful Promises for Every Woman
- The Remarkable Women of the Bible
- Small Changes for a Better Life
- A Wife After God's Own Heart
- A Woman After God's Own Heart®
- A Woman After God's Own Heart® Deluxe Edition
- A Woman After God's Own Heart®—A Daily Devotional
- A Woman After God's Own Heart® Collection
- A Woman's Call to Prayer
- A Woman's High Calling
- A Woman's Walk with God
- A Young Woman After God's Own Heart
- A Young Woman's Call to Prayer
- A Young Woman's Walk with God

Study Guides

- Beautiful in God's Eyes Growth & Study Guide
- Finding God's Path Through Your Trials Growth & Study Guide
- Life Management for Busy Women Growth & Study Guide
- Loving God with All Your Mind Growth & Study Guide
- A Mom After God's Own Heart Growth & Study Guide
- The Remarkable Women of the Bible Growth & Study Guide
- Small Changes for a Better Life Growth & Study Guide
- A Wife After God's Own Heart Growth & Study Guide
- A Woman After God's Own Heart® Growth & Study Guide
- A Woman's Call to Prayer Growth & Study Guide
- A Woman's High Calling Growth & Study Guide
- A Woman's Walk with God Growth & Study Guide

Children's Books

- God's Wisdom for Little Girls
- A Little Girl After God's Own Heart

Books by Jim & Elizabeth George

- God Loves His Precious Children
- God's Wisdom for Little Boys
- A Little Boy After God's Own Heart

Books by Jim George

- The Bare Bones Bible™ Handbook
- God's Man of Influence
- A Husband After God's Own Heart
- A Man After God's Own Heart
- The Remarkable Prayers of the Bible
- The Remarkable Prayers of the Bible Growth & Study Guide
- What God Wants to Do for You
- A Young Man After God's Own Heart

About the Author

Elizabeth George is a bestselling author who has more than four million books in print. She is a popular speaker at Christian women's events. Her passion is to teach the Bible in a way that changes women's lives. For information about Elizabeth's speaking ministry, to sign up for her mailings, or to purchase her books visit her website:

www.ElizabethGeorge.com

Toll-free: 1-800-542-4611

Elizabeth George
PO Box 2879
Belfair, WA 98528